Study Guide to

UNDERSTANDING COMPUTERS

THIRD EDITION

Rear Admiral Grace Murray Hopper
United States Navy, Retired

Professor Steven L. Mandell
Bowling Green State University

West Publishing Company

St. Paul   New York   Los Angeles   San Francisco

COPYRIGHT © 1990   by WEST PUBLISHING CO.
50 W. Kellogg Boulevard
P.O. Box 64526
St. Paul, MN 55164-1003

97 96 95 94 93 92 91 90   8 7 6 5 4 3 2 1 0

ISBN 0-314-72093-6

Contents

Preface

This study guide has been designed to accompany *Understanding Computers*, published by West Publishing Company. Throughout its development, emphasis has been placed on providing a vehicle that can assist the student in learning the text material. No design will ever take the place of conscientious student effort; however, the approaches incorporated within this study guide will make the task less difficult.

The structure of the study guide parallels the textbook. Within each chapter the student will encounter distinct segments. A chapter SUMMARY is provided at the beginning of each chapter. A series of multiple choice questions with explanatory answers has been formatted into a STRUCTURED LEARNING environment. Utilizing this technique, the student can "walk through" the material in a progressive fashion. TRUE/FALSE and MATCHING questions permit the student to obtain immediate feedback on comprehension. SHORT ANSWER exercises provide the student with an opportunity to express an understanding of the material. Solutions for odd-numbered problems are presented in the ANSWER KEY so that the student can evaluate and diagnose progress. Even-numbered solutions are in the instructor's manual. In this way, the study guide becomes an additional resource for the instructor.

The supplement to the study guide is designed to support the BASIC programming supplement found in the optional version of the text. The section structure also parallels the text material; however, a slightly different format is used. A SUMMARY is provided and a scaled-down version of STRUCTURED LEARNING is presented initially as a review mechanism. A WORKSHEET is then provided for the student to apply programming concepts and techniques. Two PROGRAMMING PROBLEMS are presented as the ultimate evaluation exercise for each section. Once again the solutions for the odd-numbered problems are incorporated into an ANSWER KEY.

Good luck!

Steven L. Mandell

Chapter 1

An Invitation to Computers

SUMMARY

As people have formed communities, they have increased their needs to gather and share information. Individuals or small families could be self-sufficient. Within communities, requirements for interdependence — and for record keeping— developed and grew.

As urbanization occurred, commerce and the need for information multiplied. During the nineteenth century, mechanization of factories led to transaction volumes that required mechanization of record keeping and computation. Inventions devised to meet these mounting needs included calculators, adding machines, the typewriter, and the cash register. Still, computational demands continued to outpace capabilities.

A major step toward modern information processing capabilities evolved to meet the challenge of the 1890 census in the United States. The U.S. Bureau of Census is required to develop a complete population survey every 10 years. After the 1880 census, it took seven-and-a-half years to compile needed statistics and reports. By 1890, the population had grown 25 percent, to some 50 million. A better method was developed by a Census Bureau employee, Dr. Herman Hollerith. Hollerith's concept: Capture data items once, in punched cards, then reuse the information indefinitely without having to transcribe and recheck accuracy. Through use of Hollerith's machines, it was possible to compile data on the 1890 census in two-and-a-half years.

Punched-card machines, which had begun to find acceptance in large business organizations, experienced explosive growth with passage of Social Security legislation. Complexity in the computation of payrolls multiplied with the need to determine employee deductions, employer contributions, and Social Security contributions.

Punched-card accounting experienced a boom. Expansion increased further during World War II, when approximately 10 million persons were inducted into the Armed Forces to present unprecedented record-keeping burdens. These and other wartime demands, such as weapons design, battlefield communications systems, and artillery ranging, stimulated research for development of computers, which came out of several laboratories immediately after World War II.

The first computer installation, fittingly, went to the Census Bureau. Business began using computers in 1952. Since then, growth has been explosive. Technologies have been applied that have reduced both the size and cost of computers. Transistors, then integrated circuits and microchips, helped reduce size, cost, and heat dissipation from electronic components. Initially, computers occupied entire rooms and buildings. Today, full-scale computers can be installed on a desktop.

One of the most important advances in computer processing was made possible by the development of "random access" storage and retrieval of information. Random access is the ability of a computer to access, change, and re-record individual data items as needed, without having to search entire files. Initially, files were recorded in sequence on punched cards or magnetic tapes. Each time information was processed, entire files had to be handled and rewritten. It was impossible for computers to support current, active business operations. Random access brought computers into the mainstream of business transactions and operations.

To qualify as a computer, a device or set of devices must be able to: 1) perform electronic processing operations that include arithmetic and comparison of values, 2) store and follow sets of instructions called programs without human intervention, and 3) communicate with people to accept inputs and deliver outputs. Computers provide technological solutions to problems and needs identified by people. Computers cannot operate entirely on their own. The value of computers depends upon the intelligence and creativity of people.

As problem-solving tools, computers meet three basic needs: volume computation, transaction processing, and information collection and reference.

The period from the early 1950s through the mid-1960s is referred to as a Computer Age. During this time, computers were used largely to process and maintain "unit records." A unit record is a collection of data items about one type of entity— for example, employee earnings records. Groups of unit records were processed as individual elements within "batch processing" systems under which it was necessary to process a complete file, in sequence, from beginning to end, each time a job was run.

Random-access techniques brought computers into the mainstream of transaction processing and operational management. Random-access methods also led to the development of massive, readily accessible files. Eventually, these files assumed an importance of their own. Sets of information reflected the status and condition of their organizations, providing models that managers could use for decision making and planning. As information resources became the main values of computer processing, an "information society" was born.

STRUCTURED LEARNING

DIRECTIONS: *First, use a blank sheet of paper to cover the answer, without reading it. Then read the question carefully and write the letter of the correct answer in the space provided. Uncover the answer to see if you chose the correct response.*

1. An "information society" consists of a working and living environment in which _____.
    a. computers are the only source of information.
    b. people are completely dependent upon computers.
    c. a minority of people have access to information sources.
    d. the majority of people depend upon information generated by computers.

    ◊ ◊ ◊ ◊ ◊ ◊ ◊ ◊ ◊ ◊ ◊ ◊ ◊ ◊ ◊ ◊ ◊ ◊

    d. the majority of people depend upon information generated by computers.

2. It is estimated that more than _____ computers are now being used in the United States.
    a. 2.5 million
    b. 10 million
    c. 20 million
    d. 2 billion

    ◊ ◊ ◊ ◊ ◊ ◊ ◊ ◊ ◊ ◊ ◊ ◊ ◊ ◊ ◊ ◊ ◊ ◊

    c. 20 million. This number is made up mostly of desktop microcomputers that have reached sales rates as high as 1 million units per month.

3. A computer can store sets of instructions known as _____ and can carry out these instructions without human intervention.
    a. procedures
    b. programs
    c. directions
    d. schedules

    ◊ ◊ ◊ ◊ ◊ ◊ ◊ ◊ ◊ ◊ ◊ ◊ ◊ ◊ ◊ ◊ ◊ ◊

    b. programs

4. For scientists, engineers, and technicians, computers provide capacity for _____, or the ability to perform large volumes of calculations rapidly and reliably.

a. transaction processing
b. number crunching
c. record keeping
d. mathematical organization

◊ ◊ ◊ ◊ ◊ ◊ ◊ ◊ ◊ ◊ ◊ ◊ ◊ ◊ ◊ ◊ ◊ ◊ ◊

    b. Number crunching; computers can perform calculations at rates of millions of operations per second.

5. The term _____ identifies a period during which methods of large-scale mass production were developed and factories were built to meet demands of growing populations.

a. Information Revolution
b. Commercial Revolution
c. Industrial Revolution
d. Technological Revolution

◊ ◊ ◊ ◊ ◊ ◊ ◊ ◊ ◊ ◊ ◊ ◊ ◊ ◊ ◊ ◊ ◊ ◊ ◊

    c. Industrial Revolution

6. Charles Babbage invented a series of mathematical processing machines, including one called the _____, which could add, subtract, multiply, and divide.

a. difference engine
b. abacus
c. adding machine
d. calculator

◊ ◊ ◊ ◊ ◊ ◊ ◊ ◊ ◊ ◊ ◊ ◊ ◊ ◊ ◊ ◊ ◊ ◊ ◊

    a. difference engine

7. In the late 1800s, Dr. Herman Hollerith developed a mechanical census tabulating machine that used _____ .

a. electronics
b. magnetic tape
c. punched cards
d. disk drives

◊ ◊ ◊ ◊ ◊ ◊ ◊ ◊ ◊ ◊ ◊ ◊ ◊ ◊ ◊ ◊ ◊ ◊ ◊

   c.   punched cards. The idea was to record information items once and be able to reuse them indefinitely.

8. The first commercial computer, the _____, was capable of performing up to 2,000 computations per second.
a. ENIAC
b. MARK IV
c. UNIVAC I
d. difference engine

◊ ◊ ◊ ◊ ◊ ◊ ◊ ◊ ◊ ◊ ◊ ◊ ◊ ◊ ◊ ◊ ◊ ◊ ◊

   c.   UNIVAC I

9. The term _____ refers to the value that information files provide to a computer-using organization.
a. transaction processing
b. information resources
c. program planning
d. volume computation

◊ ◊ ◊ ◊ ◊ ◊ ◊ ◊ ◊ ◊ ◊ ◊ ◊ ◊ ◊ ◊ ◊ ◊ ◊

   b.   information resources. Information models the status and condition of an organization to provide guidance for planning and decision making.

10. The first commercial computer system was used by the U.S. government to _____ .
a. develop radar during World War II
b. deduct Social Security taxes from workers' wages
c. assist in student program planning
d. process data for the 1950 census count

◊ ◊ ◊ ◊ ◊ ◊ ◊ ◊ ◊ ◊ ◊ ◊ ◊ ◊ ◊ ◊ ◊ ◊ ◊

   d.   The first commercial computer system was delivered to the U.S. Bureau of Census for processing of data on the 1950 population count.

TRUE/FALSE

DIRECTIONS: Read each question carefully, then circle either T or F to correctly answer each question.

1.   T   F   Computer literacy has become a basic, required capability.

2.   T   F   A computer has the ability to accept instructions or information as inputs and to deliver results, or outputs, in a form that is useful to people.

3.   T   F   The first commercial computer was developed in France by Blaise Pascal.

4.   T   F   The effort generated during the second world war gave birth to the modern electronics industry.

5.   T   F   Information resources now are seen as having values similar to a company's cash in a bank or the stocks of supplies used to create products.

6.   T   F   The first deliveries of large-scale computers began in the early 1970s.

7.   T   F   Batch processing systems allowed managers of companies to apply payroll information to the analysis of operating costs and projected profits.

8.   T   F   A unit record consists of a collection of data items about one entity.

9.   T   F   Computers could not be brought into the mainstream of operations for businesses and other organizations until a major breakthrough made possible random access storage and retrieval of information.

10. T   F   Random access storage was made possible with the invention of magnetic tape.

MATCHING

DIRECTIONS: Read each question carefully. Choose the correct answer from the list below and write the letter of the answer in the space provided.

a. random access
b. punched card
c. model
d. calculators
e. magnetic tape

f. payroll
g. cash register
h. transaction
i. assets
j. Industrial Revolution

1. A(n) _____ is a basic act of doing business.

2. One of the first mechanical _____ was invented by Blaise Pascal, who developed a machine to assist his father's work as a tax collector.

3. Through the eighteenth and nineteenth centuries, the _____ promoted increased commerce and rapid growth of cities.

4. The development of the _____ led to major changes in the retail sale of goods to consumers.

5. Information resources are regarded as _____, or valuable possessions, of an organization.

6. During the early 1950s through the mid-1960s, emphasis in the use of computers was on the same kinds of transaction processing that had been handled on _____ machines.

7. The development of _____ storage and retrieval of information made it possible to record and retrieve individual records from among massive files.

8. Prior to the invention of the magnetic disk drive, records were stored on punched cards and on _____ .

9. When the Social Security system went into operation, _____ transactions became more complex because taxes had to be calculated and deducted from employees' wages.

10. Accumulated information develops into a(n) _____ that reflects the condition and status of an organization.

SHORT ANSWER

DIRECTIONS: Read each question carefully. Answer each question using three or four complete sentences.

1. What were some of the development projects that contributed to the introduction of computers?

2. Briefly trace the development of punched card equipment.

3. How did Lady Ada Augusta, Countess of Lovelace, contribute to modern methods of computer programming?

4. Discuss the limitations associated with batch processing.

5. How did the development of the cash register affect retail sales?

6. Why can it be said that World War II gave birth to the modern elec-
    tronics industry?

7. What kinds of information can the manager of a fast-food restau-
    rant obtain by examining the sales data accumulated by a computer-
    ized system?

8. How can computers alleviate the problems of student registration
    and program planning?

9. What is meant by the term "historic processing?"

10. Describe how records are stored and retrieved with magnetic disk drives.

ANSWER KEY

True/False

1. T   **3.** F   **5.** T   **7.** F   **9.** T

Matching

1. h   **3.** j   **5.** i   **7.** a   **9.** f

Short Answer Suggested Responses

Your answers for the odd questions should contain most of the information below.

1. During World War II, the Army devised miniaturized components for the "walkie-talkie," which improved battlefield communication. Radar was invented for aircraft target identification. Research and development were undertaken for electromechanical and electronic computers to be used in artillery ranging and for research that led to the development of the atomic bomb.

3. Lady Ada Agusta devised the processing loop, an important concept that has been incorporated into modern computer programming.

5. The cash register made possible growth and departmentalization of retail stores by placing cash control at the point of sale.

7. A computerized cash register can develop information on sales by product and inventory replacement requirements, and also can keep track of sales by time of day as a basis for planning staffing levels.

9. Historic processing refers to the entry and processing of data after transactions have taken place rather than while they are happening. Batch processing is limited to the handling of historic data.

Chapter 2
Solving Problems With Computers

SUMMARY

A "computer system" is a series of interconnected devices that function in coordination to process data and develop information. The physical equipment that makes up a computer system is called "computer hardware." Computer hardware includes cabinets, devices, components, and wires.

Computer hardware itself has no ability to create and maintain information resources. To function as a tool, computers need programs that control specific types of operations. Collectively, the programs that make computers usuable are known as "software." The combination of equipment and programs (hardware and software) constitutes a "computer information system."

The process by which computer information systems are designed and implemented is known as "systems development." Systems development projects usually require the effort and talent of teams of skilled people and can involve tremendous expense.

During the late 1950s and 1960s, attempts to develop computer information systems were plagued with problems and often ended in failure. In many instances, costs overran projected budgets by millions of dollars. These same projects often took years longer to complete than was originally forecast. When information systems finally were declared ready for use, it was not unusual to discover that the technical people involved had dealt with and solved the wrong problem. In other words, the system did not deliver the expected results. In many instances, these failures were due to faulty communication between managers who needed information and computer professionals who understood the technical aspects of systems development.

Defense and space exploration provided models for managing computer systems development. The space project designed to put a man on the moon provided a useful prototype. The overall job was highly complex and involved many unknown factors. The solution was to break down the overall, complicated project into a series of predictable parts for which solutions could be devised. It then was possible to combine these separate, small solutions into a workable system.

It was recognized that this management concept could be applied successfully to the development of large computer systems. A "systems development" methodology could be based on a standard project structure. This management method breaks down a computer information systems development effort into a series of steps that can be followed in sequence to reach a planned result.

The steps in the systems development process include: identify a problem or need; define a solution; identify the resources needed to implement the solution; build an understanding among the people involved; implement; and review and revise.

The systems development process begins with the recognition that a problem exists. After the problem is defined, it is discussed by information users and "systems analysts." Systems analysts start by determining whether a computer system can solve the problem. If the decision is favorable, the project will move forward into the second step.

As a basis for any systems development effort, the prospective user must define the end results, or goals, to be achieved. User involvement and input are necessary to assure that the system attacks and solves the right problem. The systems analyst, in turn, must determine whether a computerized solution can be developed profitably. This cooperative effort of information users and systems analysts is known as a "feasibility study." Users are asked to describe, and possibly to develop samples of, the documents and reports they would require. The systems analyst gathers information to prepare a general estimate of how much the new system will cost. The user must place a value on the benefits the new system can deliver. If it is determined that the benefits outweigh the cost, in other words that the project is "cost-justified," development can proceed.

Technical effort begins with the third step, which identifies equipment and software needs for the new system. For most information systems, software will represent 50 percent or more of total startup expense. Software needs can be met by a) special, tailored programs written from scratch, or b) standard packages that can be purchased and adapted to the user's requirements. Until the 1970s, most applications were written from scratch by programmers who worked for the using organization. This process often involved prohibitive costs and several hundred working days of programming time and program testing. However, many organizations share common information system needs that can be supported by standard application packages. The use of these standard software applications, developed during the 1970s, can help to reduce the cost of application software by as much as 50 to 75 percent as compared with the writing of original programs from scratch.

The fourth step of a systems development project involves building user understanding and acceptance of the impacts and opportunities created by the new system. Users will require training to make the transition from using existing methods to using the new system competently and with confidence. The idea: The overall success and value of the new system depends upon user acceptance and implementation.

The implementation of a systems development project carries out the technical and procedural work necessary to set up an information system. Some of the tasks associated with this step are programming, equipment installation, preparing sample data to test the new programs, actual testing of programs, and training of users. Then, the complete system is tested under procedures that reflect actual working conditions. From the information user's standpoint, the most significant aspect of the implementation step involves setting up the files that will support use of the new system.

As business conditions change and users identify new opportunities, the system will need modifications and enhancements. Therefore, as a final step in the systems development project, one or two review sessions are held after the system is in place and is being used on a regular basis. The first of these sessions is used to identify opportunities for improvements to be made to the new system. The second review, generally held three to six months after a new system has been put into operation, provides an opportunity to identify improvements that should be made within the organization's systems development procedures themselves.

STRUCTURED LEARNING

DIRECTIONS: *First, use a blank sheet of paper to cover the answer, without reading it. Then read the question carefully and write the letter of the correct answer in the space provided. Uncover the answer to see if you chose the correct response.*

1. The combination of equipment, such as cabinets, devices, components, and wires, is known collectively as _____ .
a. electronics
b. computer software
c. computer hardware
d. a computer information system

◊ ◊ ◊ ◊ ◊ ◊ ◊ ◊ ◊ ◊ ◊ ◊ ◊ ◊ ◊ ◊ ◊ ◊ ◊

c. computer hardware. Hardware includes all equipment related to operation of a computer.

2. To function as a tool, computers need programs that control specific types of operations. Collectively, these programs are known as _____ .
a. equipment
b. computer software
c. computer hardware
d. a computer information system

◊ ◊ ◊ ◊ ◊ ◊ ◊ ◊ ◊ ◊ ◊ ◊ ◊ ◊ ◊ ◊ ◊ ◊

    b.   computer software. The programs that make computers usable are known as software.

3. In most cases, if an organization has been performing the same tasks in the same manner for _____ year(s) or longer, it probably is time to change.
a.   one
b.   three
c.   five
d.   seven

◊ ◊ ◊ ◊ ◊ ◊ ◊ ◊ ◊ ◊ ◊ ◊ ◊ ◊ ◊ ◊ ◊ ◊

    c.   five years. Technology quickly outdates information handling capabilities.

4. The procedures, equipment, facilities, and information resources necessary to put computers to productive use can be incorporated into a project structure known as _____ .
a.   programming
b.   unbundling
c.   data processing
d.   systems development

◊ ◊ ◊ ◊ ◊ ◊ ◊ ◊ ◊ ◊ ◊ ◊ ◊ ◊ ◊ ◊ ◊ ◊

    d.   systems development. Developing a computer system involves a major, high-cost effort.

5. Generally, the first step in the development of computer information systems is to _____.
a.   identify a problem or need
b.   identify the resources needed to implement the solution
c.   build an understanding among the people involved
d.   set schedules

◊ ◊ ◊ ◊ ◊ ◊ ◊ ◊ ◊ ◊ ◊ ◊ ◊ ◊ ◊ ◊ ◊ ◊

    a.   identify a problem or need. A statement of user requirements and objectives forms the framework for the system that is developed.

6. Professionals who specialize in the design and development of computer information systems are known as _____.
a. managers
b. systems analysts
c. technicians
d. information users

◊ ◊ ◊ ◊ ◊ ◊ ◊ ◊ ◊ ◊ ◊ ◊ ◊ ◊ ◊ ◊ ◊ ◊ ◊

b. systems analysts. These people require both technical knowledge and application background.

7. The first major result of a feasibility study is the identification of _____.
a. user expectations
b. needed resources
c. software requirements
d. system implications

◊ ◊ ◊ ◊ ◊ ◊ ◊ ◊ ◊ ◊ ◊ ◊ ◊ ◊ ◊ ◊ ◊ ◊ ◊

a. user expectations. Goals for a computer information system are defined by the information outputs required by users.

8. Until the 1970s, most applications, such as the university information system described in this chapter, were _____.
a. written by computer technicians
b. written from scratch by programmers who worked for the using organization
c. written by systems analysts hired by the using organization
d. purchased and adapted to the individual requirements of the using organization

◊ ◊ ◊ ◊ ◊ ◊ ◊ ◊ ◊ ◊ ◊ ◊ ◊ ◊ ◊ ◊ ◊ ◊ ◊

b. written from scratch by programmers who worked for the using organization

9. Many organizations share common information system needs, such as payroll and general accounting, that can be supported by standard software application packages. If a using organization can find a suitable, standard application package, the cost of programs can be reduced by as much as _____.

a. 10 to 20 percent
b. 30 to 40 percent
c. 50 to 75 percent
d. 80 to 90 percent

◊ ◊ ◊ ◊ ◊ ◊ ◊ ◊ ◊ ◊ ◊ ◊ ◊ ◊ ◊ ◊ ◊ ◊ ◊

    c.   50 to 75 percent. These savings result from eliminating the detailed task of writing program code from scratch.

10. In the long run, success and value of an information system lie with acceptance and use of the new methods by _____ .
a. computer technicians
b. systems analysts
c. company managers
d. information users

◊ ◊ ◊ ◊ ◊ ◊ ◊ ◊ ◊ ◊ ◊ ◊ ◊ ◊ ◊ ◊ ◊ ◊

    d.   information users. Operational computer information systems ultimately belong to their users.

TRUE/FALSE

DIRECTIONS: *Read each question carefully, then circle either T or F to correctly answer each question.*

1. T F The combination of computer hardware and software constitutes a computer information system.

2. T F Computer systems development should be approached as a purely technical undertaking rather than as a management challenge.

3. T F In today's business climate, change is said to be the only constant.

4. T F A feasibility study involves a cooperative effort by a responsible information user and a systems analyst to define the problem and to determine whether it is solvable with the aid of computers.

5. T F The purpose of a cost-benefit analysis is to determine if the benefits predicted for a system justify the costs that will be encountered to develop it.

6.   T   F   In most projects that develop information systems, software will represent less than one-third of the total start-up expense.

7.   T   F   At present, nearly all application software packages are developed and supplied by computer equipment manufacturers.

8.   T   F   It frequently is necessary to modify or adapt standard software programs to meet an organization's specific needs.

9.   T   F   Information systems should be redesigned or revised before development is concluded to accommodate new goals and last-minute improvements.

10. T   F   The primary goal of systems development is to create and provide information resources to meet identified needs.

MATCHING

DIRECTIONS: *Read each question carefully. Choose the correct answer from the list below and write the letter of the answer in the space provided.*

a. interactive   f. files
b. customers   g. prototype
c. systems analyst   h. programs
d. creeping commitment i. obsolete
e. microcomputers   j. software packages

1.   Computers have been identified as devices that process data and develop information resources by accepting input and following sets of instructions in stored _____ .

2.   The 1960s project designed to put a man on the moon before the end of the decade served as a(n) _____ for devising practical methods of managing computer system development.

3.   If an organization's information system is more than five years old, there is a good chance it is _____.

4.   A system that permits students to register for classes through on-line terminals is known as _____ .

5.   Many organizations share common information system needs that can be supported by standard _____ .

6. The tremendous success of _____ is due primarily to the availability of universally applicable, inexpensive software packages.

7. A(n) _____ is usually responsible for developing technical specifications, determining what software is available, and estimating the costs involved in developing, buying, and/or adapting the needed programs.

8. An approach to system development in which managers monitor the system development process step by step, and commit money and time in stages as benefits and values are established, has been referred to as implementing a(n) _____ .

9. An information system's _____, or users, should conduct the final tests of the new system before it is put into operation.

10. From a standpoint of the information user, the most significant part of the implementation step lies in setting up the _____ that will support use of the new system.

SHORT ANSWER

DIRECTIONS: *Read each question carefully. Answer each question using three or four complete sentences.*

1. Thomas J. Watson, Jr., a former president of the IBM Corporation, stated that no computer could do anything that people couldn't do with a pencil and paper. What is the main problem with this statement?

2. Why is user involvement essential to effective systems development?

3. What are the purposes and advantages of a step-by-step approach to systems development?

4. Why is it beneficial for systems analysts and computer technicians to have some understanding of business procedures, and for businesspeople to have an understanding of some of the technical aspects of computers and information systems?

5. What similarities do management of space exploration programs share with management of computer systems development?

6. Identify the six basic steps of the standard systems development process.

7.   What is a feasibility study and what main purpose does it serve?

8.   Why does system development begin with definition of outputs?

9.   What is meant by the term "unbundling?" How has unbundling affected the computer industry?

10. What are the purposes of reviews conducted after a system has been implemented?

ANSWER KEY

True/False

1. T   **3.** T   **5.** T   **7.** F   **9.** F

Matching

1. h   **3.** i   **5.** j   **7.** c   **9.** b

Short Answer Suggested Responses

Your answers for the odd questions should contain most of the information below.

1. It is true that pencil and paper methods can achieve the same results. However, the computer does the work faster and with greater assurance of accuracy because of the self-checking features of programs. Also, the computer does not grow weary of repetitive tasks the way people do.

3. A step-by-step approach to systems development permits check-pointing to monitor projected results and costs. Projects are structured so that commitments for the major expenses of a system are withheld until the design and feasibility have been tested and supported both by users and computer system specialists.

5. Similarities center around the nature of both kinds of projects. They are complex and involve dealing with unknowns. The strategy is to break down massive projects into a series of smaller parts that can be understood and managed.

7. A feasibility study aims at determining the nature of a problem and identifying a projected solution. Then, the projected solution is evaluated to determine whether the procedures will work and how much implementation will cost. The costs then are compared with the value of benefits projected by users. The value of the benefits must equal or exceed the costs.

9. Unbundling was the result of a consent decree that resolved an antitrust suit against IBM. The commitment was to market hardware and software separately. The effect upon the market was to launch an entire new industry that concentrates upon software development.

Chapter 3
The Machine Itself:
Processing and Storage Hardware

SUMMARY

Computers process data and deliver information by performing a series of steps, or functions. This sequence of steps is called the "information processing cycle." The steps in the information processing cycle are input, processing, output, and storage.

The devices that make up a computer system support these functions; each piece of equipment is designed to carry out specific operations related to processing data and delivering information to people.

Input devices convert data items from human-readable form into codes that can be handled and processed by computers. This coding is called machine language. Captured data items are entered, or read, into a computer in preparation for processing. Input accuracy is critical. Once captured, data items are reused indefinitely. Thus, if an item is wrong, the entire system can be affected and its value degraded.

Processing takes place in a portion of a computer known as the central processing unit (CPU). The CPU directs operation of and communication between all devices that comprise a computer system. The CPU consists of three parts that function in close coordination: the control unit, the arithmetic/logic unit (ALU), and primary storage. The ALU and the control unit function together as the processor. The control unit interprets instructions and gives commands for their execution. The ALU manipulates data, performing arithmetic (addition, subtraction, multiplication, division) and logic (comparison) operations. The primary storage unit within the CPU holds program instructions and data in support of processing operations. Primary storage is generally located on separate circuit boards from the processor.

A computer processes data by coding information in binary notation. Numbers, letters, and other characters are represented by sequences of binary 1 and 0 (on and off) values. A computer's binary notation system is known as its machine language. A computer's machine language establishes the proper electronic states, either on or off, for the recording and processing of instructions and data items. Two coding systems are used by the majority of computers and for exchange of information among computers through communication channels: the American Standard Code for Information Interchange (ASCII) and the Extended Binary Coded Decimal Interchange Code (EBCDIC).

Computer processing involves a series of ultra-simple operations carried out at ultra-high speeds. A computer performs two basic functions: addition and comparison. Addition and electronic polarity switching make possible the equivalent of full calculation capabilities. Subtraction is negative addition, multiplication is repeated addition (at rates of millions of functions per second), and division is repeated negative addition (subtraction). A computer also is capable of comparing a stored value with an input value and determining whether the two values are equal or unequal, or whether one is greater than, not greater than, less than, or not less than the other. Based on the results of these comparisons, the computer selects the next processing sequences or data items to be processed.

Output devices deliver information to users in human-readable form or store the information for future use. Video screen displays and printed documents are two of the most common forms of output.

Computers are equipped with two kinds of storage capabilities: primary and secondary. Primary storage, also called "main memory," is a device within the CPU that provides direct operational support through storage of programs and data. Primary storage is volatile; contents are erased when power is removed. By contrast, secondary storage is long-term and potentially permanent. Secondary storage devices record large volumes of data items and programs that are swapped into primary storage for processing.

One of the techniques computers use to assure accuracy is to add an extra bit, called a parity bit, to bytes of data that are stored and processed. Computers can be set up for either odd parity or even parity. As the computer processes data, it checks for an odd or even number of 1 bits in each byte. Another accuracy check, which is used primarily to verify account or identification numbers, is known as the check-digit method. With this method, a number is appended to an identification number for validation purposes. A series of computations is applied to digits within the identification number when it is entered for processing. The last digit of the computation result is compared with, and must be equal to, the check digit.

Computer processing functions include classify, sort, calculate, summarize, and store. A "classify" function identifies data items according to meaningful characteristics. A "sort" function arranges data items into a desired sequence. A "calculate" operation applies arithmetic computations or logic operations to one or more numeric values. The "summarize" capability of a computer develops totals for groups of values. The "store" function causes the computer to record, or write, needed information onto secondary storage devices.

The main method used to form primary storage devices is known as random-access memory (RAM). RAM is a volatile, nonpermanent form of memory used for storing instructions and data for processing. RAM can be read over and over without being destroyed. However, new instructions or data may be written over existing items.

Read-only memory (ROM) is a permanent form of storage used for microprogramming (series of instructions for carrying out frequently required functions). These are devices that store recorded items continuously, even when the computer is turned off. When a computer is turned on, the ROM program causes the computer to check out its RAM units and all the devices within the system, including secondary storage units and printers, to make sure that they are in working order and can communicate with the processor's control unit.

Programmable read-only memory (PROM) is a programmable version of ROM. (It can be programmed only once, however). ROM programs can be varied using erasable programmable read-only memory (EPROM) chips. Users can erase and reprogram EPROM chips with special devices that use ultraviolet light.

Access to data held in secondary storage can be either direct or sequential, depending on the recording materials, or media, that are used. Sequential storage is used primarily for backup files. The most common medium for sequential storage is magnetic tape. Large volumes of information can be stored on a single tape. Magnetic tape provides an inexpensive storage medium and can be erased and reused many times. Because magnetic tape is a sequential medium, however, the entire content of a tape must be read each time a tape is processed. For this reason, the use of tape is unsuitable for direct support of current business operations.

The main method of providing direct access to secondary storage devices is through use of magnetic disk media. Magnetic disks make possible direct, or random, access to individual records and, because of this capability, are able to support current operations of a business. A disk drive erases existing data items when they are processed and rewritten; therefore, it is necessary to store the original data items for future reference and for backup use in the event of system failure. Magnetic disks and disk drives are more expensive than tapes and tape drives.

Other storage media include mass-storage devices and laser storage. Mass-storage devices can store vast amounts of data at comparatively lower equipment costs, and generally are used for historic or other information that users want to have available for occasional reference. Laser storage works by focusing high-intensity light beams upon plastic-coated metal disks. The laser records data by burning a series of pits into the surface of the disk. To read this data, the positions of these pits are decoded to produce text and graphic images. Initially, laser recordings were permanent, Currently, however, laser devices are being developed that provide both reading and writing capabilities.

STRUCTURED LEARNING

DIRECTIONS: *First, use a blank sheet of paper to cover the answer, without reading it. Then read the question carefully and write the letter of the correct answer in the space provided. Uncover the answer to see if you chose the correct response.*

1. Computers process data and deliver information by running through a series of steps, or functions. This sequence of steps is known as the _____.
a. input and output cycle
b. operational sequence
c. information processing cycle
d. function sequence

◊ ◊ ◊ ◊ ◊ ◊ ◊ ◊ ◊ ◊ ◊ ◊ ◊ ◊ ◊ ◊ ◊ ◊

c. information processing cycle. The steps in this cycle are input, processing, output, and storage.

2. Data items are converted from human-readable form into codes that can be handled and processed by computers. The coding used to control internal operations within a computer is called _____.
a. computer language
b. computer coding
c. data coding
d. machine language

◊ ◊ ◊ ◊ ◊ ◊ ◊ ◊ ◊ ◊ ◊ ◊ ◊ ◊ ◊ ◊ ◊ ◊

d. machine language. Each make and model of computer has its own machine language.

3. The two basic processing functions a computer performs are _____.
a. input and output
b. processing and storage
c. addition and comparison
d. multiplication and division

◊ ◊ ◊ ◊ ◊ ◊ ◊ ◊ ◊ ◊ ◊ ◊ ◊ ◊ ◊ ◊ ◊ ◊

c. addition and comparison. Repeating operations and reversing polarity make possible full arithmetic capabilities. Comparisons provide a computer's logic capabilities.

4. Computer processing is performed entirely by setting a series of circuits and devices to on or off conditions. This kind of processing is known as _____.
a. two-state processing
b. on and off processing
c. primitive arithmetic
d. binary arithmetic

◊ ◊ ◊ ◊ ◊ ◊ ◊ ◊ ◊ ◊ ◊ ◊ ◊ ◊ ◊ ◊ ◊ ◊

d. binary arithmetic. Binary means two. To input and output decimal values, a computer performs internal conversions.

5. The _____ directs the communication and coordination of operations between the CPU and other devices that form a computer system.
a. control unit
b. arithmetic/logic unit
c. processor
d. microprocessor

◊ ◊ ◊ ◊ ◊ ◊ ◊ ◊ ◊ ◊ ◊ ◊ ◊ ◊ ◊ ◊ ◊ ◊

a. control unit. All instructions are interpreted and their execution is initiated through the control unit.

6. The _____ unit within the CPU holds program instructions and data in support of processing operations.
a. secondary storage
b. primary storage
c. control unit
d. arithmetic/logic unit

◊ ◊ ◊ ◊ ◊ ◊ ◊ ◊ ◊ ◊ ◊ ◊ ◊ ◊ ◊ ◊ ◊ ◊

b. primary storage. All instructions are entered and all outputs are routed through primary storage.

7. The method used to access data in primary storage devices is known as _____.
a. random-access
b. nondestructive read
c. sequential storage
d. read-only

◊ ◊ ◊ ◊ ◊ ◊ ◊ ◊ ◊ ◊ ◊ ◊ ◊ ◊ ◊ ◊ ◊ ◊ ◊

a.   random-access. Under random access, records can be found as they are needed to support transactions as they occur.

8.   Special programs that check out the computer circuits and input operating system programs are stored in _____.
a.   random-access memory
b.   batch processing
c.   read-only memory
d.   primary storage

◊ ◊ ◊ ◊ ◊ ◊ ◊ ◊ ◊ ◊ ◊ ◊ ◊ ◊ ◊ ◊ ◊ ◊ ◊

c.   read-only memory. ROM programs start the process of "booting" a computer.

9.   _____ has the same general meaning as random access and refers to the computer's ability to find, process, and re-store individual records, as they are needed, at any time.
a.   Read-only memory
b.   Direct access
c.   Sequential access
d.   Primary storage

◊ ◊ ◊ ◊ ◊ ◊ ◊ ◊ ◊ ◊ ◊ ◊ ◊ ◊ ◊ ◊ ◊ ◊ ◊

b.   Direct access. This term means the computer can go directly to each needed record.

10.   Microcomputers and some input devices use flexible acetate platters coated with iron oxide known as diskettes or _____.
a.   floppy disks
b.   read/write heads
c.   mass-storage devices
d.   tape reels

◊ ◊ ◊ ◊ ◊ ◊ ◊ ◊ ◊ ◊ ◊ ◊ ◊ ◊ ◊ ◊ ◊ ◊ ◊

a.   floppy disks. Diskettes can be used both for direct processing support and for backing up files kept on hard disks.

TRUE/FALSE

DIRECTIONS: *Read each question carefully, then circle either T or F to correctly answer each question.*

1.   T   F   The quality and reliability of information produced depends upon the accuracy of the input provided to a computer information system.

2.   T   F   A computer performs two basic functions: binary arithmetic and addition.

3.   T   F   The contents of secondary storage are destroyed when a computer is turned off or power is interrupted for any other reason.

4.   T   F   Some computers are able to communicate with sounds that imitate the human voice.

5.   T   F   Secondary storage devices tend to have higher capacities and lower costs than primary storage.

6.   T   F   The arithmetic/logic unit (ALU) manipulates and stores data.

7.   T   F   Logical operations involve comparisons for equality or lack of equality between two values.

8.   T   F   Digital computers must convert human-readable items into binary form before processing can take place.

9.   T   F   A "classify" function arranges data items into a desired sequence, such as the arrangement of student records in alphabetic order according to last names.

10.   T   F   Disk files can support current operations of a business because of their ability to find and alter files directly, during transaction processing.

MATCHING

DIRECTIONS: *Read each question carefully. Choose the correct answer from the list below and write the letter of the answer in the space provided.*

a.   sequential
b.   processor
c.   random access
d.   bytes
e.   swapping

f.   output
g.   logic
h.   functions
i.   main memory
j.   branches

1.   Computers process data and deliver information by running through a series of steps, or _____.

2. Based on the comparison of two values, the computer selects the next processing sequences, or program _____.

3. _____ hardware delivers information to users in human-readable form or stores the information for future use.

4. The control unit and arithmetic/logic unit, together, often are referred to as the _____.

5. _____ operations involve comparisons for equality among two values.

6. Primary storage is also known as _____.

7. The shifting of program instructions and data items between primary and secondary storage is known as _____.

8. A series of bits, usually eight, is used to represent a letter, number, or special character. These eight-bit codes are known as _____.

9. The term _____ describes a basic capability for storing and finding data items individually, without having to process entire files in sequence.

10. Magnetic tape is suited ideally for applications that normally are handled through _____ processing techniques.

SHORT ANSWER
DIRECTIONS: Read each question carefully. Answer each question using three or four complete sentences.

1. Identify and describe the steps in the information processing cycle.

2. Describe the two related functions that input devices perform.

3. Explain the addition function of a computer.

4. Explain the comparison function of a computer.

5. What features distinguish primary storage from secondary storage?

6. What is the role of the central processing unit (CPU)?

7. Describe the check-digit method used by computers to assure accuracy in processing.

8. What purpose does the "summarize" capability of a computer serve? How can the manager of a fast-food restaurant benefit from a computer's ability to summarize data?

9. What is meant by the term "nondestructive read/destructive write?"

10. What are some of the advantages magnetic disk can provide, as compared with magnetic tape?

ANSWER KEY
True/False
1. T   3. F   5. T   7. T   9. F

Matching
1. h   3. f   5. g   7. e   9. c

Short Answer Suggested Responses
Your answers for the odd questions should contain most of the information below.

1. The steps in the information processing cycle: 1) input, or entry of source data and capture in machine-readable form; 2) processing, or manipulation through combining or computation upon data items; 3) output, or delivery of results in human-usable form; and 4) storage, retention of information for continuing use.

3. A computer performs addition through the manipulation of on-off functions of binary circuits. Addition is the only basic arithmetic function performed by a computer. The other functions result from repetition or changes in electrical values. Subtraction is negative addition. Multiplication is repeated addition. Division is repeated subtraction.

5. Primary storage is in microchips; secondary storage usually is on magnetic media. Primary storage is high speed, volatile, and expensive. Secondary storage is comparatively slow, permanent, and relatively inexpensive.

7. Check-digit verification is used for identification or account numbers. A final digit is appended to the base number. A series of computations is performed on the base number and the final digit in the answer must match the check digit. This method catches account number entries in which digits have been transposed or entered incorrectly.

9. Nondestructive read/destructive write describes operation of a typical disk drive. A record is read nondestructively. This means the record is transferred to memory without removing the information from the disk. Destructive write means that, when the record is rewritten to the disk file, the new information is over-written on the old and the old information is destroyed. Memory devices also operate with nondestructive read and destructive write.

Chapter 4
The Machine Itself:
Input and Output Hardware

SUMMARY

Input devices are the tools people use to communicate and interact with computers. Input operations are designed to enter data into a computer so that processing can take place. Input can be completed in a single step or through a two-step process. Under a single-step procedure, an operator enters data at an interactive terminal. The computer validates data items as they are being entered, then updates the file. Word processing performed on a microcomputer is an example of single-step input. Under two-step input, data items are captured in an initial procedure, but do not affect the files of a system. This provides an opportunity to check the accuracy of the entries before altering the files. In the second step, the captured items are processed to update the data files.

A number of different media are used for input operations. The earliest practical method of data input was the punched card. Data are entered into punched cards through a keyboard on a keypunch machine. The data items can be validated by listing and checking control totals or by using a verifier machine. When the data items have been verified, the cards are fed into high-speed machines that read the information into computer memory. Punched cards can serve as "turnaround documents." For example, punched cards can be used to tag products kept in inventory. Then, when the products are used or sold, the cards can be input to update inventory records maintained by computers. Utility companies can use punched cards to bill customers and then process customer payments.

More efficient electronic media have almost completely eliminated the use of punched cards for large-scale data capture and input applications. Some of the newer methods include key-to-magnetic media input devices that capture data directly onto magnetic tape, tape cassettes, disks, or diskettes. The data entries are edited by the computer or verified by checking the video display. After the data items have been verified, the magnetic tape or disk is mounted on a secondary storage unit for high-speed input.

The great majority of delays, errors, and problems occur during the input phase. To reduce the problem, a number of source-data automation methods have been developed to increase the speed and reliability of data input. These methods also are known as "interactive input." Users work at remote input-output devices known as terminals. The users communicate with the computer through a keyboard. In turn, the computer communicates with the user through a display screen. Terminals also can be placed at points where they may be operated by users or customers. At a university, for example, interactive terminals linked into the main campus computer can be used to support registration activities. Some interactive terminals are used to capture transaction data items from product labels or tags at the point of sale. This method, known as "direct input," is used extensively by supermarkets and other large retail stores.

The universal product code (UPC) is one of the coding systems used by retailers and suppliers to mark product labels. The UPC code consists of a series of bars and spaces between that represent numeric values. When the code is read by laser beams or processed through fiber-optic devices, the computer responds by providing the price, description, and other product information associated with that code. The information may be printed on a receipt and also displayed at the sales counter. Transaction information is captured in the computer and can be used for status reporting and inventory management.

Another source-data automation technique is to mark documents so that they can be read by devices attached to computers. Examples include magnetic ink character recognition (MICR) and optical character recognition (OCR). MICR uses ink containing iron particles to record symbols on checks and deposit slips. The coding, which indicates customer account numbers, bank identification, and dollar amounts, is magnetized and then read by machines called reader-sorters. Optical character recognition (OCR) devices recognize the shapes and patterns of letters, numbers, and symbols. The data is read by passing a beam of light over the imprinted text. The characters are recognized through sensing of positions of the lines that form them.

Sensor input is achieved by linking computers to automatic machines or processing systems. For example, oil refineries use processing equipment to determine temperatures, times, and other conditions to assist in chemical analysis and product development. The sensors on this equipment input this data directly into a computer. Using other methods, computers are capable of assisting in the design and manufacture of products. Under computer-assisted design (CAD) techniques, product specifications, such as performance or dimension requirements, are entered into a computer. The computer responds by presenting a picture of the product to be developed. This design is then used to control machines that actually manufacture the new product. This application is known as computer-assisted manufacturing (CAM).

In other applications, input can be completed through the display screen. One through-the-screen input method permits the user to select applications or services by touching points on a computer-generated display. Graphics input can be accomplished by using a device called a "light pen" to draw images on the screen for direct computer processing. Other graphics input devices include the "graphics tablet," a flat, board-like device on which the user draws with a pointed device resembling a pencil, and the "scanner," which scans an image electronically from a paper or acetate original and transfers the picture to computer memory.

Voice recognition input devices permit users to communicate with computers by speaking into a microphone. At present, the computer can identify and process a relatively limited number of words. Over time, however, the vocabulary computers can recognize is expected to increase.

Output devices make it possible for people to use and receive information from computers. The two primary methods of computer output are displays and documents. Displays are temporary outputs that are used and then erased. The cathode ray tube (CRT) is the most common display output. A terminal that uses a CRT is often referred to as a "video display terminal" or VDT. Output images also can be displayed electronically using light-emitting diodes (LED) and through liquid crystal display (LCD) units. Stadium scoreboards are an example of LED display. Digital wristwatches and laptop computers frequently use liquid crystal displays.

Printers produce relatively permanent document outputs by imprinting information and images on paper. Printed documents are often referred to as "printouts" or "hard copy." A number of different types of printers are available for use with computers. "Draft-quality" printers produce legible printouts that can be used within an organization. The most common draft-quality printer is the "dot-matrix printer." For improved print quality, some dot-matrix printers can make multiple imprints to produce "near-letter-quality" documents. "Letter-quality" printers use plastic or metal printing elements to make physical impressions of characters. Letter-quality printouts are comparable in quality to documents prepared on typewriters. "Non-impact" printers include thermal printers and ink-jet printers.

To meet high-speed output requirements, line printers and page printers can be used. Line printers are generally used with medium- and large-scale computers. Commonly used line printers include print-wheel printers, chain printers, and drum printers. Page printers are the fastest method for producing hard copy. Page printers, also called laser printers or xerographic printers, use copier technology to produce full-page outputs in a single operation.

In addition to displays and printers, outputs also can be delivered through a number of special-purpose devices. One device, which produces hard copies of graphic images, is the "plotter." Plotters can be used to create lines, curves, bar charts, maps, and other useful graphics by moving a pen-like device, called a stylus, over paper. Another output technique produces computer-output microfilm by photographing documents to deliver reduced-sized photographic images. Microfilm uses less storage space and is more durable than paper documents. The film can be read on special projection devices or can be enlarged through photography or xerography to create paper documents.

Other methods of output include audio output, video output, and control signals. Audio output involves delivering information to users in sequences of sounds that resemble the human voice. Video output can generate full-color, drawing-quality images using computer graphics capabilities. Animation programs can create animated output sequences on film or videotape. Control signals are a form of computer output that operates, or controls, other systems or devices. Examples range from factory automation to household applications used to monitor heating and air conditioning.

Computers come in a wide range of sizes and capacities. The general categories, from smallest to largest, include microcomputers, minicomputers, mainframe computers, and supercomputers. The "microcomputer" uses a microprocessor on a single chip as its CPU. Microcomputers are also known as desktop computers and personal computers. "Minicomputers" provide full computer capacities and capabilities at the fraction of the cost of a large-scale system and can be used to support supermarket, retail store, and university applications. "Mainframe computers," considered to be "large scale," can process program instructions approximately 20 times faster than microcomputers, and have vast primary and secondary storage capacities. "Supercomputers" typically have productive capacities that are at least double those of mainframes. They are extremely expensive and generally are used by only the largest organizations.

STRUCTURED LEARNING

DIRECTIONS: *First, use a blank sheet of paper to cover the answer, without reading it. Then read the question carefully and write the letter of the correct answer in the space provided. Uncover the answer to see if you chose the correct response.*

1. The _____ functions of a computer make it possible for computers to interact with people, and for people to use and receive information from computers.
a.   processing and storage
b.   input and output
c.   display and document
d.   edit and verification

◊ ◊ ◊ ◊ ◊ ◊ ◊ ◊ ◊ ◊ ◊ ◊ ◊ ◊ ◊ ◊ ◊ ◊ ◊

    b.   input and output. Accuracy verification during input is critically important to system quality.

2. Most delays, errors, and problems occur during the _____ phase of the information processing cycle.
a.   input
b.   output
c.   processing
d.   storage

◊ ◊ ◊ ◊ ◊ ◊ ◊ ◊ ◊ ◊ ◊ ◊ ◊ ◊ ◊ ◊ ◊ ◊

    a.   input. Human error is the greatest problem in system opera-
        tion.

3. When computers first were introduced, _____ were virtually the
only practical method for data input.
a. magnetic tapes
b. magnetic disks
c. punched cards
d. coding systems

◊ ◊ ◊ ◊ ◊ ◊ ◊ ◊ ◊ ◊ ◊ ◊ ◊ ◊ ◊ ◊ ◊ ◊

    c.   punched cards. Early computers functioned within punched
        card accounting systems.

4. An input method which uses devices that recognize the shapes and
patterns of actual letters, numbers, and symbols is known as _____ .
a. magnetic ink character recognition (MICR)
b. universal product code (UPC)
c. optical character recognition (OCR)
d. computer-assisted design (CAD)

◊ ◊ ◊ ◊ ◊ ◊ ◊ ◊ ◊ ◊ ◊ ◊ ◊ ◊ ◊ ◊ ◊ ◊

    c.   optical character recognition (OCR).

5. With interactive input methods, workers handle transactions by
operating remote computer input-output devices known as _____ .
a. processors
b. keyboards
c. display screens
d. terminals

◊ ◊ ◊ ◊ ◊ ◊ ◊ ◊ ◊ ◊ ◊ ◊ ◊ ◊ ◊ ◊ ◊ ◊

    d.   terminals. Another term is "on-line" operation.

6.   _____ devices are the tools that computers use to communicate results of processing to people.
a.   Input
b.   Output
c.   Storage
d.   Graphics

◊ ◊ ◊ ◊ ◊ ◊ ◊ ◊ ◊ ◊ ◊ ◊ ◊ ◊ ◊ ◊ ◊ ◊

    b.   Output. Displays and documents are the main output forms.

7.   The electronic devices used to form images by illuminating positions on a matrix or grid are known as _____ .
a.   liquid crystal displays (LCD)
b.   video display terminals (VDT)
c.   optical character recognition (OCR)
d.   light-emitting diodes (LED)

◊ ◊ ◊ ◊ ◊ ◊ ◊ ◊ ◊ ◊ ◊ ◊ ◊ ◊ ◊ ◊ ◊ ◊

    d.   light-emitting diodes (LED). Displays on many electric clocks and appliances use light-emitting diodes.

8.   The most commonly used draft-quality printer is the _____ .
a.   thermal printer
b.   laser printer
c.   dot-matrix printer
d.   ink-jet printer

◊ ◊ ◊ ◊ ◊ ◊ ◊ ◊ ◊ ◊ ◊ ◊ ◊ ◊ ◊ ◊ ◊ ◊

    c.   dot-matrix printer. These units produce draft-quality documents.

9.   A _____ is a drawing device that produces outputs by driving pen-like units.
a.   plotter
b.   daisy wheel
c.   scanner
d.   touch screen

    a.   plotter.

10. Microcomputers that use microprocessors as their CPUs, and include co-processors that expand data-handling capabilities are known as _____ .

a.   mainframe computers
b.   minicomputers
c.   supercomputers
d.   supermicrocomputers

    d.   supermicrocomputers. These units are called workstations and often are linked into data networks.

TRUE/FALSE

DIRECTIONS: *Read each question carefully, then circle either T or F to correctly answer each question.*

1.   T   F   Word processing uses single-step input.

2.   T   F   Because of their high storage capacities, punched cards are used for large-scale data capture and input applications.

3.   T   F   Data entry traditionally has been the weakest link within the information processing cycle.

4.   T   F   It is possible to capture the text of entire books using optical character recognition (OCR) readers.

5.   T   F   The idea of interactive input is to capture information directly into computers at the time when transactions take place.

6.   T   F   Terminals that rely on a central computer for processor and memory support generally are called "intelligent terminals."

7.   T   F   The most common display output is achieved with light-emitting diodes.

8.   T   F   Thermal printers and ink-jet printers are two types of "impact printers."

9.   T   F   Line printers are used primarily with microcomputers.

10.   T   F   Microfilm can be used as an output medium for graphic images as well as for data documents.

MATCHING

DIRECTIONS: Read each question carefully. Choose the correct answer from the list below and write the letter of the answer in the space provided.

a.   verifiers
b.   reader-sorters
c.   display
d.   optical character
     recognition (OCR)
e.   voice synthesizers

f.   computer-output microfilm
g.   turnaround documents
h.   video display terminal
i.   direct input
j.   universal product code (UPC)

1.   Under _____ methods, data capture and data entry are combined in a single operation.

2.   The _____ , a bar coding system used by retailers and suppliers to mark product labels, can be read by fiber-optic devices or laser readers built into checkstands.

3.   The accuracy of punched card content can be checked by using machines called _____ .

4.   Punched cards used both to bill customers and to credit payments are known as _____ .

5.   Bank documents, such as checks and deposit slips, encoded with ink containing magnetic particles can be read by machines called _____ .

6.   _____ is a data coding system which uses devices that recognize the shapes and patterns of actual letters, numbers, and symbols.

7.   A terminal that includes a cathode ray tube (CRT) is often called a _____ .

8.   The shared characteristic of all _____ devices is that they are temporary.

9.   Electronic units that generate sounds resembling human speech are known as _____ .

10. Many organizations alleviate the storage problems associated with paper documents by using _____ .

SHORT ANSWER
DIRECTIONS: *Read each question carefully. Answer each question using three or four complete sentences.*

1. Describe the two-step input process.

2. How are punched cards used as "turnaround documents?"

3. Why is data entry considered the weakest link within the information processing cycle?

4. How do direct input methods input data to computers?

5.   What characteristics distinguish dumb and intelligent terminals?

6.   How do dot-matrix printers create imprints?

7.   List, from smallest to largest, the general categories used to describe computers.

8.   What basic equipment units make up a plotter?

9.   What are the key features of a supermicrocomputer?

10.   What are the common denominators that define a microcomputer?

ANSWER KEY

True/False

1. T   3. T   5. T   7. F   9. F

Matching

1. i.   3. a.   5. b.   7. h.   9. e.

Short Answer Suggested Responses

Your answers for the odd questions should contain most of the information below.

1.   Under two-step input, entries are recorded, or captured, into a storage medium, but do not impact the files of a system. This provides an opportunity to check the accuracy of the data entries before the files are altered. Then, as the second step, the captured items are processed to update the data files.

3.   The great majority of delays, errors, and problems occur during the input phase. This is because system users can make mistakes during data entry or enter the wrong data. Once input has been completed, electronic processing methods take over to handle the storage, processing, and output phases quickly and reliably.

5. Dumb terminals, which may consist of just a keyboard and a display, rely on a central computer for processing, storage, and output capabilities. Intelligent terminals typically have their own processing, secondary storage, and printing capabilities.

7. The general categories used to describe computers, from smallest to largest, include microcomputers, minicomputers, mainframe computers, and supercomputers.

9. Supermicrocomputers use microprocessors as their CPUs. In addition, many supermicrocomputers include "co-processors" that expand data-handling capabilities. Some co-processors increase mathematical capabilities. Others specialize in the control of databases. Supermicrocomputers have extensive memory and storage capabilities which surpass the needs of typical office applications. Network integration capabilities also are included.

Chapter 5
How Computers Communicate Information

SUMMARY

The devices attached to computers to support their operations are called "peripherals." Included are secondary storage units, as well as input and output devices. To direct operations, a computer sends and receives signals to and from its own peripherals. Computers also use peripherals to communicate with terminals, other computers, or with external systems and equipment. For this kind of communication to occur, the computer must bridge greater distances than those involved in operating its own peripherals.

The same kinds of equipment and communication channels can be used to send signals between computers that are located at distances as close as the other side of a room or as far away as another continent. To send and receive messages over distances, computers must use telecommunication networks and technologies. The term "data communication" describes this blending of computer and telecommunications capabilities.

For hundreds of years, people have sought ways to communicate information over distances. Throughout the centuries, people have devised increasingly sophisticated methods of transmitting information. These methods include the use of drums, smoke signals, flags, flashing lights, and the Morse telegraph. Prior to the introduction of computers, networks of telegraph offices and teletypewriters were used for such purposes as transmitting news items and conducting stock transactions.

With the advent of random-access disk drives, businesses began handling orders on an interactive basis. The next logical step was to link computers through use of telecommunication networks and equipment. This capability would allow computers to communicate with other computers and receive input from distant terminals. Two major technical problems frustrated this effort. First, computers are digital, DC devices while telephone networks operate on analog, AC circuits. Telephone circuits were designed to carry the continuous tones of voice communication, while computers were designed for stop-start, binary operation. A second obstacle lay in differences of data coding formats.

The telecommunications industry had standardized many years ago on ASCII coding. The computer industry was committed largely to EBCDIC code, the standard for large IBM systems.

Devices were developed in the 1960s that translated codes and transmitted signals compatibly. These devices, positioned between computers and telephone circuits, perform the basic functions "modulation" and "demodulation." During modulation, the direct-current (DC) pulses from computers are converted to alternating-current (AC) wave patterns that can be handled on analog channels. Demodulation is the reverse process.

Today, telephone companies and long distance carriers are the main providers of communication channels for computer users. A "communication channel" is a pathway used to carry data or voice transmissions from one location to another. Computers linked to telephone instruments make it possible to transmit data through the same basic steps followed to make a telephone call. Organizations also can set up their own wires, cables, or electronic links to establish a private communication capability.

The primary types of channels available for transmission of data include telegraph lines, telephone lines, coaxial cables, microwave links, communication satellites, laser beams, and fiber-optic cables.

A telegraph line uses a single strand of wire that connects two points. Early telegraph signals generally were transmitted through strands of wire that ran beside railroad tracks. Trained operators decoded the series of clicks that made up Morse code. Communication took place in one direction at a time. Before computers increased demands, teletypewriters used telegraph lines to transmit information at a rate of about 60 words per minute. The computerized teletypewriter circuits currently in use can carry approximately 1,200 words per minute.

Telephone lines use two carriers, or a pair of wires, to send and receive signals at the same time. This means that two people can talk at once or two data transmission points can be sending and receiving at the same time. Telephone lines have a one-way transmission capacity of more than 1,200 words per minute.

A coaxial cable is a high-grade transmission link with multiple wires and an ultra-wide transmission capacity, or "bandwidth." Data can be transmitted at rates of millions of bits per second. Coaxial cables are used to link mainframe computers to secondary storage and other high-speed peripherals. Television signals also are transmitted over coaxial cables.

A microwave link transmits and receives signals over high-frequency radio waves. Microwaves provide a high-quality communication link because they are not affected by weather or other kinds of radio interference. Microwaves have extremely wide bandwidths, in the same general range as coaxial cables. Because they travel in straight lines, and therefore cannot follow the curvature of the Earth, microwave signals must be relayed every 90 to 100 miles. This limitation is overcome through the use of communication satellites. Microwave signals are sent to the satellites which travel in stationary orbit above Earth. Satellites relay the signals to Earth stations that are distant from the original point of transmission. These links permit worldwide communication with microwaves.

Laser beams can be directed over distances and can serve as communication channels. Laser beams, which travel in straight lines, generally are used for data transmission over short distances.

Fiber-optic cables are composed of thin strands of glass, each about the thickness of a human hair. They transmit both voice and data through optical digital signals. Full cables of fiber-optic strands can carry hundreds of times more data and voice traffic than conventional copper coaxial cables. The quality of voice transmission is much higher with fiber-optic cables than with conventional channels that use copper cables.

"Modems," which take their name from the terms "modulate" and "demodulate," are the devices used to transmit computer-generated data over telephone lines. A modem performs the basic function of interfacing a computer with a communication channel and converting signals from digital-to-analog and back from analog-to-digital formats. Modems are available in a number of sizes, capacities, and configurations.

Most of the data communication units in use today are called "smart modems." Smart modems come with their own software that uses the computer's CPU and storage capabilities to add special features for data communication operations. Smart modem software can automatically answer the telephone linked into a computer to receive data transmission. In many cases, the computer also can be instructed to place telephone calls and transmit messages when the receiving computer answers its telephone.

Systems that interconnect multiple computers and/or user input/output stations are called "networks." Networks can be local, regional, national, or worldwide in scope. Most networks represent variations or mixtures of three basic configurations, or "topologies." These are bus, ring, and star. A "bus" network is a data communication network supported by a direct, high-speed link to the processor of a central computer. A "ring" network is composed of a series of nodes connected to one another along a continuous circular path. A message passes to all nodes in the network until it reaches its destination. In a "star" network, all nodes are linked into a central computer switch. This switch controls receipt and delivery of all messages.

Networking capabilities have been used to create a number of services called "information utilities." These services provide information of value to an identified group of users. Users with modem-equipped computers can access the information. The utility's computer monitors usage and may charge for services. In some instances, the utility may provide information at no charge. Organizations which maintain information utilities include governmental agencies, news organizations, public libraries, banks, investment companies, and airlines.

"Bulletin boards" are another network-based service. A bulletin board is a service that allows users to post messages for viewing by callers. Callers can review the notices, then access or retrieve files to meet their needs. Some bulletin boards are available to any user with a microcomputer, a modem, and a telephone. Others are reserved for the use of certain individuals or professional groups. Users must have special identification codes to access these systems.

Information utilities and bulletin boards provide information resources that are external to a computer-using organization. Internal information resources are central computer files available to authorized users. For example, these files may contain sales figures or information regarding the financial status of a company. Generally, these files are accessed through terminals or microcomputers linked into a local area network. Communication can occur both to and from the central computer. Entering information into a database for inclusion in stored files is known as "uploading." When users retrieve information from a central computer into a microcomputer it is called "downloading."

STRUCTURED LEARNING

DIRECTIONS: *First, use a blank sheet of paper to cover the answer, without reading it. Then read the question carefully and write the letter of the correct answer in the space provided. Uncover the answer to see if you chose the correct response.*

1. The combination of computer and telecommunications capabilities is known as _____ .
a.   communication processing
b.   teleconnections
c.   data communications
d.   telephonic transmission

◊ ◊ ◊ ◊ ◊ ◊ ◊ ◊ ◊ ◊ ◊ ◊ ◊ ◊ ◊ ◊ ◊ ◊

   c.   data communications. Transmission between computers rival conversation between people for use of communication networks.

2. A(n) _____ is a high-grade, multiple-wire transmission channel used on mainframe computers to link the processor to secondary-storage units and other high-speed peripherals.
a.   microwave link
b.   fiber-optic cable
c.   acoustic-coupler modem
d.   coaxial cable

◊ ◊ ◊ ◊ ◊ ◊ ◊ ◊ ◊ ◊ ◊ ◊ ◊ ◊ ◊ ◊ ◊ ◊

   d.   coaxial cable. These carriers can transmit millions of bits per second.

3. A(n) _____ is a communication carrier comprised of multiple, thin strands of glass that carry signals as light waves.
a. microwave link
b. fiber-optic cable
c. acoustic-coupler modem
d. coaxial cable

◊ ◊ ◊ ◊ ◊ ◊ ◊ ◊ ◊ ◊ ◊ ◊ ◊ ◊ ◊ ◊ ◊ ◊

b. fiber-optic cable. Fiber-optic cables provide both high-quality and high-speed transmission.

4. The term _____ identifies a process for converting direct-current (DC) pulses from computers to alternating-current (AC) wave patterns that can be handled on analog channels.
a. modulate
b. translate
c. transmission
d. conversion

◊ ◊ ◊ ◊ ◊ ◊ ◊ ◊ ◊ ◊ ◊ ◊ ◊ ◊ ◊ ◊ ◊ ◊

a. modulate. Modulation is signal conversion. Demodulation returns the signals to their original state.

5. An external modem with a plug-in connection to a computer is called a(n) _____ .
a. internal modem
b. direct-connect modem
c. indirect-connect modem
d. acoustic-coupler modem

◊ ◊ ◊ ◊ ◊ ◊ ◊ ◊ ◊ ◊ ◊ ◊ ◊ ◊ ◊ ◊ ◊ ◊

b. direct-connect modem. These modems link communication parts and telephone lines.

6. A _____ permits sharing of workloads and secondary storage files by managers and workers within a single office or building.
a. communication satellite
b. local-area network
c. switch
d. node

◊ ◊ ◊ ◊ ◊ ◊ ◊ ◊ ◊ ◊ ◊ ◊ ◊ ◊ ◊ ◊ ◊ ◊

b.   local-area network. LANs can share data in "file server" peripherals.

7.   "Store-and-forward" message services are generally associated with _____ network topologies.
a.   bus
b.   ring
c.   star
d.   satellite

◊ ◊ ◊ ◊ ◊ ◊ ◊ ◊ ◊ ◊ ◊ ◊ ◊ ◊ ◊ ◊ ◊ ◊ ◊

c.   star. A star network has a central, switching computer that is linked directly to all user nodes. The central computer must have capacity to implement electronic mail capabilities.

8.   A _____ network is supported by a direct, high-speed link to the processor of a central computer.
a.   bus
b.   ring
c.   star
d.   direct link

◊ ◊ ◊ ◊ ◊ ◊ ◊ ◊ ◊ ◊ ◊ ◊ ◊ ◊ ◊ ◊ ◊ ◊ ◊

a.   bus. A bus is present within the internal structure of most computers. The bus links controllers for peripherals directly to the CPU.

9.   Money to cover consumer purchases is transferred automatically from the buyer's account to the seller's through an application known as _____ .
a.   consumer automation
b.   automatic debiting
c.   electronic mail
d.   electronic funds transfer (EFT)

◊ ◊ ◊ ◊ ◊ ◊ ◊ ◊ ◊ ◊ ◊ ◊ ◊ ◊ ◊ ◊ ◊ ◊ ◊

d.   electronic funds transfer (EFT). EFT systems also handle transactions between banks.

10. The entry of information into a central computer from a terminal is called _____ .

a. uploading

b. upgrading

c. downloading

d. downgrading

◊ ◊ ◊ ◊ ◊ ◊ ◊ ◊ ◊ ◊ ◊ ◊ ◊ ◊ ◊ ◊ ◊ ◊

a. uploading. When a central computer delivers data to a terminal, this is known as "downloading."

TRUE/FALSE

DIRECTIONS: *Read each question carefully, then circle either T or F to correctly answer each question.*

1. T F Today's business, governmental, commercial, defense, transportation, and many other systems could not exist without data communication links.

2. T F On telephone lines, communication takes place along a pair of wires in only one direction at a time.

3. T F Telegraphic lines have a far greater transmission capacity, or bandwidth, than telephone lines.

4. T F Laser beams typically are used to transmit data over long distances.

5. T F Fiber-optic techniques have brought the same kinds of improvements to communication channels as compact discs have delivered for audio recordings.

6. T F A modem installed within a computer itself is called an "internal modem."

7. T F Data transmission speeds often are measured in "baud," a term derived from Baudot, the name of a French telecommunication pioneer.

8. T F A "node" can be a dumb terminal, a smart terminal, or a full-scale computer system.

9. T F A ring network is one of the most sophisticated and costly network configurations.

10. T F A "log" is a copy of the content of all messages handled within a network.

MATCHING

DIRECTIONS: *Read each question carefully. Choose the correct answer from the list below and write the letter of the answer in the space provided.*

a.	acoustic-coupler modem	f.	switch
b.	topology	g.	downloading
c.	microwave link	h.	node
d.	workstation	i.	digital
e.	smart modem	j.	analog

1. Telephone circuits were originally designed for the transmission of _____ signals.

2. Computer systems were designed to process _____ signals, a series of stop-start pulses carried by direct current.

3. A(n) _____ is a communication channel that transmits and receives signals through use of high-power, short wavelength, radio signals carried through the air.

4. A(n) _____ is a modem that comes with its own software that can add special features such as telephone calling and answering.

5. A(n) _____ is a modem that can input communications signals and receive transmitted signals through a telephone handset.

6. Each point linked into a network with capabilities for entry or receipt of data is known as a(n) _____ .

7. A small terminal designed specifically to support job requirements of an individual user is called a(n) _____ .

8. A computer used specifically to transfer messages from sending to receiving nodes and to monitor operations is called a(n) _____ .

9. The specific configuration used to assemble a network is called its _____ .

10. The retrieval of information from a central computer to a terminal or microcomputer is known as _____ .

SHORT ANSWER

DIRECTIONS: *Read each question carefully. Answer each question using three or four complete sentences.*

1.   What two technical incompatibilities had to be overcome before communication could occur between computers?

2.   List the seven primary types of channels available for transmission of data that are described in this chapter.

3.   What are "half-duplex" and "full-duplex" transmission?

4.   What is a "communication satellite?"

5.   Why are laser beams used for data transmission limited primarily to short distances?

6.   What advantages do fiber-optic cables have over other types of transmission channels?

7.   How are bus-type links used *within* computers?

8.   How do messages move through a ring network?

9.   What is an "information utility?"

10.   How can information utilities assist health-care professionals?

ANSWER KEY
True/False
1. T   3. F   5. T   7. T   9. F

Matching
1. j   3. c   5. a   7. d   9. b

Short Answer Suggested Responses

Your answers for the odd questions should contain most of the information below.

1. The two obstacles involved transmission signal and information coding incompatibilities. The transmission-signal problem was simply that telephone lines operated with AC analog signals and computers used DC digital transmission. The information coding obstacle centered around the fact that ASCII coding had been the standard of telecommunications industry while EBCDIC, developed for IBM computers, was the most-used format for information coding on computers.

3. Under half-duplex transmission, a telegraph line can transmit signals in either direction—but only in one direction at a time. Telephone lines use two carriers, or a pair of wires, for full-duplex service. Under full-duplex transmission, two people can talk at once or two data transmission points can be sending and receiving at the same time.

5. The use of laser beams is limited because there is concern that the infrared radiation of laser beams may be dangerous to human health. Laser beams also travel in straight lines and, therefore, must be relayed through line-of-sight transmission.

7. Within a computer, a bus is a high-speed channel into which working components of a hardware system are linked. Microcomputers generally use a single bus to link the circuit boards that control all of the working parts of a system. The circuit boards that plug into the bus control the processor, memory, video controller, disk controller, and printer connections.

9. An information utility is an organization that makes files of information available for use by members or subscribers who access the information through modem-equipped computers. The users may pay fees based on usage, or the information may be provided by a nonprofit organization to students, scientists, or others at no charge.

Chapter 6
Controlling Computers:
System and Application Software

SUMMARY

Software encompasses all the programs that control operation of a computer. Programs are the sets of instructions that guide computers in processing data and delivering information required by users. The selection and/or development of software is critical: the lack of the proper software tools can inhibit the effectiveness and efficiency of an information system. Moreover, it is common for overall software costs to exceed those for equipment.

To make computer capabilities available, the user must enter two basic kinds of software: system software and application software. System software encompasses all of the programs that make equipment available and also direct processing required by users. The main groups of programs within a system software package include: operating system, utility programs, status-checking programs, productivity tools, and programming languages.

An operating system is a set of programs that the computer uses to manage its own operations. Operating systems control execution of applications. This eliminates the computer down time formerly devoted to setup activities by human operators. Operating systems increase productivity further by establishing processing priorities and allocating memory and other resources. The operating system reads the labels on the files stored in disk drives and uses this information to create a directory of files. This directory enables the software to find, retrieve, process, and update the content of needed files.

Utility programs are system software modules that provide processing services common to many users. Some common needs met by utility programs are disk formatting; erasing programs and data from disks; and sorting, copying, and moving file content. Some utility programs provide support for standard services, including file management, input, and output. Because these services are provided by programs already existing in the operating system, disk storage space is conserved and processing is faster.

Status-checking programs are utility modules that help a user to verify the condition of a disk device and its ability to record data. These software tools also can help maintenance personnel to diagnose problems as a basis for repairs.

Productivity tools improve the effectiveness and efficiency of computers and the people who use them. Software modules that support such capabilities as virtual storage and multiprocessing are known as productivity tools. "Virtual storage" enables a computer to treat a portion of secondary storage as an extension of primary storage. Programs held in secondary storage can be accessed without special retrieval and memory-allocation operations. "Multiprocessing" software makes possible the coordinated use of two or more separate CPUs for sharing of workloads. Workloads are shared to realize the best total processing output for all of the linked systems.

System software also includes a series of language translator programs. These programs convert programming instructions, or "source code," written by people into machine language, or "object code," used by computers for processing. The development of programming languages has increased the value and effectiveness of computers as problem-solving tools.

The first stored programs for computer processing were written in "low-level" or machine language. Programmers wrote instructions with 0 and 1 notations for each command to be executed. Programming in machine language was a difficult and expensive task. The first improvement in programming techniques came with the introduction of "assembly languages." Assembly languages made it possible for programmers to use alphabetic commands to specify computer operations. However, the programmer still had to write one instruction for each operation performed by the computer and to allocate storage space for all items to be processed.

The development of "high-level" languages further improved program-writing capabilities. High-level languages apply "macro" instructions, or single program commands that cause a computer to execute an entire sequence of operations. At present, hundreds of high-level programming languages are available. Among the most widely used are COBOL, FORTRAN, PL/1, BASIC, APL, Pascal, Ada, and RPG.

An application program is a set of instructions written in a programming language that controls the execution of a user job. Development and implementation of application programs is among the most vital and costly requirements connected with the productive use of computers. Program development generally relies on a widely accepted approach known as "structured programming." Four key methodologies form the basis for structured programming techniques: top-down design, documentation, program testing, and the chief programming team (CPT) approach.

"Top-down design" provides a framework for the planning, writing, and testing of programs in steps. This method defines the major elements, or modules, of the program first, then expands into more detailed steps later. "Documentation" encompasses all of the instructions and descriptions that help people to understand, maintain, and use programs. This should include an actual listing of the program code. "Program testing" involves the creation of sets of data that replicate the processing that the program is to perform. Test data also is executed to check the design and operating integrity of the individual program modules and the system as a whole. The "chief programming team" approach breaks down the work of program writing into manageable tasks. A CPT typically is comprised of a small number of programmers working under the supervision of a chief programmer, who oversees program development.

Most application programs can be developed through use of one of three approaches: the user can purchase ready-to-use application packages; the programs can be developed under user control through use of databases and a fourth-generation language (4GL); or the programs can be written from scratch and coded in high-level languages.

An "application package" consists of all the materials needed to implement an application. These can include programs, instruction manuals, and possibly special devices to be installed in computers. Application packages can be purchased by individual users from numerous software store chains. Application packages are used by businesses to support common needs such as payroll, billing, accounts receivable, and financial reporting. Word processing, data management, and spreadsheet preparation are the three major types of microcomputer application.

In many instances, users can access needed information through the use of "query languages" or "fourth-generation languages (4GL)." A query language consists of a special vocabulary that inexperienced users can apply to retrieve items from a database and carry out specific processing functions. Query commands are based on everyday English terms such as GET, DISPLAY, ADD, MOVE, COMPUTE, PRINT, LIST, and SORT. By entering a sequence of these commands, the user, in effect, can achieve the same results as a program. Fourth-generation languages (4GL) are software tools with advanced query-language capabilities. A 4GL enables the user to link a series of query-language commands for automatic execution. In some situations, the use of 4GLs may simplify and reduce the cost of program development.

In some cases, project teams determine that it is best to write programs from scratch in a programming language. Writing code in programming languages remains a necessary activity within the computer industry. Application packages, for example, start as custom-written programs. To develop a program for a new application, a program-development process generally is followed. Although the pattern may vary from one organization to another, the series of steps followed in program development include defining the problem; designing a solution; writing the program; and compiling, debugging, and testing the program.

STRUCTURED LEARNING

DIRECTIONS: First, use a blank sheet of paper to cover the answer, without reading it. Then read the question carefully and write the letter of the correct answer in the space provided. Uncover the answer to see if you chose the correct response.

1. The term _____ encompasses all of the programs that make computer equipment available to users and direct processing.
   a. computer hardware
   b. system software
   c. operating system
   d. utility program

◊ ◊ ◊ ◊ ◊ ◊ ◊ ◊ ◊ ◊ ◊ ◊ ◊ ◊ ◊ ◊ ◊ ◊

   b. system software. System software is a kind of intermediary between users and the functions performed by computers.

2. The original idea for the development of operating systems was to _____ .
   a. improve productivity
   b. enlarge secondary storage capacities
   c. decrease status-checking requirements
   d. increase printing speeds

◊ ◊ ◊ ◊ ◊ ◊ ◊ ◊ ◊ ◊ ◊ ◊ ◊ ◊ ◊ ◊ ◊ ◊

   a. improve productivity. Operating systems were developed to eliminate the computer down time devoted to setup activities by human operators.

3. On minicomputer and larger systems, the operating system has the capacity to process multiple jobs concurrently through a capability known as _____ .
   a. status checking
   b. virtual storage
   c. multiprocessing
   d. multiprogramming

◊ ◊ ◊ ◊ ◊ ◊ ◊ ◊ ◊ ◊ ◊ ◊ ◊ ◊ ◊ ◊ ◊ ◊

   d. multiprogramming. The system software performs the "housekeeping" needed to switch back and forth among multiple application programs.

4.   _____ are system software modules that provide processing services common to many user applications such as disk formatting and sorting, copying or moving file content.
a.   Supervisor modules
b.   Productivity tools
c.   Utility programs
d.   Command programs

◊ ◊ ◊ ◊ ◊ ◊ ◊ ◊ ◊ ◊ ◊ ◊ ◊ ◊ ◊ ◊ ◊ ◊

   c.   Utility programs. Many application programs call up and rely on utility modules.

5.   A(n) _____ is a set of instructions that controls the execution of a user job.
a.   command program
b.   virtual storage program
c.   application program
d.   DIR program

◊ ◊ ◊ ◊ ◊ ◊ ◊ ◊ ◊ ◊ ◊ ◊ ◊ ◊ ◊ ◊ ◊ ◊

   c.   application program. Application programs adapt general-purpose computers to create special tools for users.

6.   A list of steps that describes the processing to be performed in a program is known as a(n) _____ .
a.   job queue
b.   directory
c.   algorithm
d.   module

◊ ◊ ◊ ◊ ◊ ◊ ◊ ◊ ◊ ◊ ◊ ◊ ◊ ◊ ◊ ◊ ◊ ◊

   c.   algorithm. To illustrate, a recipe for baking a cake is an algorithm.

7.   The majority of application programs are written in _____ .
a.   assembly languages
b.   query languages
c.   low-level languages
d.   high-level languages

◊ ◊ ◊ ◊ ◊ ◊ ◊ ◊ ◊ ◊ ◊ ◊ ◊ ◊ ◊ ◊ ◊ ◊ ◊

    d.   high-level languages. The languages can be understood by people and executed by computers.

8. _____ , a standardized and comprehensible language, is the most popular business programming language.

a.   FORTRAN
b.   COBOL
c.   BASIC
d.   PL/1

◊ ◊ ◊ ◊ ◊ ◊ ◊ ◊ ◊ ◊ ◊ ◊ ◊ ◊ ◊ ◊ ◊ ◊ ◊

    b.   COBOL (COmmon Business-Oriented Language). COBOL has special strengths for creating and maintaining files.

9. The programming language _____ was developed for use with time-sharing systems that support multiple users concurrently.

a.   Ada
b.   Pascal
c.   BASIC
d.   APL

◊ ◊ ◊ ◊ ◊ ◊ ◊ ◊ ◊ ◊ ◊ ◊ ◊ ◊ ◊ ◊ ◊ ◊ ◊

    c.   BASIC. BASIC has been particularly popular for use with microcomputers.

10. Writing instructions in a programming language is known as _____ .

a.   coding
b.   branching
c.   debugging
d.   initialization

◊ ◊ ◊ ◊ ◊ ◊ ◊ ◊ ◊ ◊ ◊ ◊ ◊ ◊ ◊ ◊ ◊ ◊ ◊

    a.   coding. Effective program writing benefits from the planning and control applied by structured programming methods.

TRUE/FALSE

DIRECTIONS: Read each question carefully, then circle either T or F to correctly answer each question.

1. T F Within a computer system, the cost of software seldom exceeds the cost of equipment (hardware).

2. T F The operating system can create a directory that enables the software to find, retrieve, process, and update the content of needed files.

3. T F The first stored programs were written in high-level languages.

4. T F An "application," in data processing vocabulary, is an individual job performed by a computer.

5. T F Top-down design employs a "modular" approach that breaks down a problem into smaller and smaller sub-problems.

6. T F A chief programming team (CPT) generally includes a chief programmer, a backup programmer, and a librarian.

7. T F FORTRAN is the oldest high-level programming language.

8. T F Packaged programs come ready-to-use and, therefore, never require any special adaptation or preparation before systems can be implemented.

9. T F "Simple sequence" logic involves executing instructions one statement after another, in the order presented by the program.

10. T F Logic errors can be difficult to find because locating them requires extensive retracing of the steps in the underlying design of the program.

MATCHING

DIRECTIONS: Read each question carefully. Choose the correct answer from the list below and write the letter of the answer in the space provided.

a. queue
b. operating system
c. debugging
d. command program
e. compiler

f. loop
g. system software
h. flowcharting
i. branch
j. backup copies

1. To make computer capabilities available, the user must enter two basic kinds of software into a computer: _____ and application software.

2. The _____ keeps track of the equipment units that make up a computer system.

3. When a computer is turned on and prepared for service, the supervisor module, or _____ , is the first software loaded.

4. The job control program is designed to identify user applications and to establish and manage a job _____ , or lineup of work to be performed.

5. One important use of the COPY capability is to create _____ of secondary storage files for use if the originals are damaged or destroyed.

6. The process of locating, isolating, and resolving errors within a program is known as _____ .

7. _____ is a graphic method which can be used to represent the processing steps in a program through a set of connected symbols.

8. The _____ processing pattern allows the computer to repeat the same instructions again and again, as long as given conditions prevail.

9. The _____ processing pattern allows the computer to bypass statements in a program.

10. A(n) _____ is a programming-language translator for a specific language that accepts code written by a programmer and generates machine-language instructions.

SHORT ANSWER

DIRECTIONS: *Read each question carefully. Answer each question using three or four complete sentences.*

1. Why is software considered the "agent" of the user within the computer system?

33

2. List the five main groups of programs within a system software package, as described in this chapter.

3. Initially, how did the development of operating systems improve computer productivity?

4. What are COPY and MOVE operations?

5. What is a "macro instruction?"

6. List the three approaches available for the acquisition of application software, as described in this chapter.

7. What are the three major types of microcomputer application?

8. What four key methodologies are used to distinguish structured-programming methods?

9. What four steps are generally followed to create an application program?

10. What are "syntax errors" and "logic errors."

ANSWER KEY

True/False

1. F   3. F   5. T   7. T   9. T

Matching

1. g   3. d   5. j   7. h   9. i

Short Answer Suggested Responses

Your answers for the odd questions should contain most of the information below.

1. Software serves the user by interpreting and carrying out instructions that are entered through a keyboard or input through application programs.

3. Before operating systems were developed, each time a job was to be run, the computer was shut down and cleared of the programs and files for the previous job, then set up again from scratch. Human operators loaded the application programs, mounted the secondary storage files, and set up the printers. Operating systems were developed to eliminate the computer down time devoted to setup activities by human operators.

5. A macro instruction causes the computer to execute an entire sequence of steps in response to a single command.

7. The three major types of microcomputer application that have formed a multi-billion-dollar market include word processing, data management, and spreadsheet preparation.

9. The series of steps followed in program development include: define the problem; design a solution; write the program; and compile, debug, and test the program.

Chapter 7
Microcomputer Software:
Word Processing, Data Management,
And Spreadsheets

SUMMARY

The key to mastering the use of microcomputers lies in understanding capabilities of software application packages. Software application packages enable users with no previous computer experience to put computers to work immediately— and with ease. Three main types of software applications have led to widespread acceptance of microcomputers: word processing, data management, and spreadsheet application packages.

The term "word processing" identifies computerized systems designed for input, processing, storage, and output of "text" documents. Microcomputers have proven ideal tools for word processing because of the flexibility and low cost of diskette storage. Diskettes containing text files can be stored together with the documents themselves.

The main application for word-processing software is business correspondence. In addition, businesses use word-processing applications for price quotations, proposals, and legal documents. Medical personnel use word-processing applications for patients' medical charts. Students use word processors to generate term papers.

The first word-processing packages followed a "command" design approach. Comand-driven word-processing programs require the user to enter special commands within the body of the text to control formatting, and the selection of type styles and spacing. "Menu-driven" systems began replacing command-type programs in the early 1980s. Menu-driven systems enable the user to select desired functions from special displays (menus). Function keys on the computer keyboard can be assigned to control formatting and other operations.

Menu-driven software applications are more "user friendly." The operator can learn the application in less time because there is no need to memorize large sets of commands. Menu-driven packages are interactive. Selecting certain menu options will cause the computer to present a second set of choices on a "submenu" or "prompt screen." A prompt screen asks for specific control-type entries. Selecting a printing operation, for example, may cause the computer to present a detailed prompt screen requesting the user to enter margin, page-length, spacing, and other format control information.

Some word-processing packages are "file oriented," others are "page oriented." A file-oriented package stores the complete text of a document as a single unit in memory. A page-oriented system keeps only one page of a document in memory at a time. Processing from memory is faster with file-oriented systems; however, users must store and protect their own work at frequent intervals. A page-oriented system provides greater protection: Each page is saved automatically when the next page is started.

The first steps taken to produce a text document involve creating a file to store the input and getting the text into the computer. In most instances, text capture is accomplished by keying the text on a keyboard. Text entry is generally faster with a word processing computer than a typewriter because of the computer's ability to start new lines automatically. This capability is known as "word wrap."

Text editing is easier on a word processor than with traditional typewriting methods. Corrections and revisions can be made through use of editing functions such as cursor movement, strikeover, insert, delete, move and copy, search, and search/replace.

Format specifications control the appearance of a printed document. The user can enter settings to specify margin size, spacing, type style, and other elements, or these specifications may be left at the default setting provided by the software developer. Under some software packages, the appearance of the text displayed on the screen differs from how the document will appear when printed. Some users prefer programs with screen formatting capabilities. With these programs, the text appears on the screen exactly as it will appear in printed document form. This capability is known as WYSIWYG, which stands for "What you see is what you get." Word-processing applications commonly use draft, letter-quality, and laser printers.

Power-typing applications use computer capabilities to personalize mass-produced form letters. This can save businesses a substantial amount of time and money. Advertising and customer service are two of the main applications for power typing.

Word-processing programs must have capabilities for recording files on storage devices, copying files from one disk to another, and deleting unneeded files from storage devices. The two general types of software packages that can be used to implement file-management needs are "file managers" and "database management systems (DBMS)."

A file manager is a program that deals with individual files; the software can be used to create, change, and use only one set of records. File-manager software cannot interrelate the content of multiple files. A database management system is software that permits access to and control of information stored in multiple files by multiple application programs.

A database that interrelates the information contained in multiple files is called a "relational database." A database that contains current information that represents the condition and status of an organization functions as an "information model" that managers can use to monitor operations and make business projections.

DBMS software makes extensive use of menu and prompt screens. The screens guide users through the procedures involved in setting up file structures and entering data into files. Entering complete sets of records into a database can be a major undertaking; for each file, the user must identify and name every data element. For each data element, the user must specify the size and type of data. However, once the DBMS is implemented, it can add efficiency for the organization and productivity for individual workers.

Preparation of spreadsheets is a major responsibility for managers in business and other organizations. Physically, a spreadsheet simply is a wide document organized into columns and rows for the presentation of data. Data entries are made into points where the columns and rows intersect. These locations are known as "cells." The figures in the cells are calculated by using formulas to produce totals. Most spreadsheets are used to report financial information or to project future financial status.

Spreadsheet software provides two main advantages over manual methods for preparation of these reports. First, under instruction from the user, the computer can calculate the data values automatically. In addition, spreadsheet software enables the user to make unlimited changes and corrections without detracting from the appearance of the finished document.

From the standpoint of software design and application, there are significant differences between routine data communication applications and bulletin board operations. Data communication software generates the signals sent and received through use of modems and public telecommunication channels. In addition to the communication requirements for answering telephones and for transmitting messages to callers, bulletin boards must be able to receive, file, and make information available automatically under control of special software.

STRUCTURED LEARNING

DIRECTIONS: *First, use a blank sheet of paper to cover the answer, without reading it. Then read the question carefully and write the letter of the correct answer in the space provided. Uncover the answer to see if you chose the correct response.*

1. The term "word processing" identifies computerized systems designed for input, processing, storage, and output of _____ .
a. data items
b. text documents
c. spreadsheet documents
d. budget projections

◊ ◊ ◊ ◊ ◊ ◊ ◊ ◊ ◊ ◊ ◊ ◊ ◊ ◊ ◊ ◊ ◊ ◊

b.   text documents. Businesses prepare billions of letters and other documents each month. Word-processing methods help to reduce costs and increase productivity.

2.   It usually takes less time to learn how to use a menu-driven application than a command-driven application. This is because menu-driven applications _____ .
a.   eliminate the need to memorize large sets of commands
b.   display the commands in the top portion of the screen
c.   do not provide as many options as command-driven applications
d.   have default settings which cannot be altered

◊ ◊ ◊ ◊ ◊ ◊ ◊ ◊ ◊ ◊ ◊ ◊ ◊ ◊ ◊ ◊ ◊ ◊

a.   The operator can learn to use a menu-driven application in less time because it no longer is necessary to memorize large sets of commands.

3.   When they are using a file-oriented word processing program, users are instructed to save their files to disk _____ .
a.   on a weekly basis
b.   at the end of each work day
c.   two or three times per day
d.   about every 15 minutes

◊ ◊ ◊ ◊ ◊ ◊ ◊ ◊ ◊ ◊ ◊ ◊ ◊ ◊ ◊ ◊ ◊ ◊

d.   about every 15 minutes. If power is disrupted while a document is in work, the entire content of memory is lost.

4.   The cursor is moved within a document through use of the _____ , PgUp, PgDn, Home, and End keys.
a.   F10
b.   ESC
c.   arrow
d.   numeric keypad

◊ ◊ ◊ ◊ ◊ ◊ ◊ ◊ ◊ ◊ ◊ ◊ ◊ ◊ ◊ ◊ ◊ ◊

c.   Pressing the arrow keys will cause the cursor to move in the direction indicated on the key—up, down, left, or right.

5. The Delete key and/or the _____ key commonly are used to remove text from word processing documents.

a. F10

b. ESC

c. Backspace

d. arrow

◊ ◊ ◊ ◊ ◊ ◊ ◊ ◊ ◊ ◊ ◊ ◊ ◊ ◊ ◊ ◊ ◊ ◊

c. Backspace. The Backspace key removes only one character at a time.

6. A _____ operation removes text from one location in a document and places it in another.

a. move

b. copy

c. delete

d. strikeover

◊ ◊ ◊ ◊ ◊ ◊ ◊ ◊ ◊ ◊ ◊ ◊ ◊ ◊ ◊ ◊ ◊ ◊

a. move. The move operation is like cut-and-paste editing.

7. The basic structure for storage and use of data is the _____ .

a. data item

b. file

c. record

d. document

◊ ◊ ◊ ◊ ◊ ◊ ◊ ◊ ◊ ◊ ◊ ◊ ◊ ◊ ◊ ◊ ◊ ◊

b. file. Files become the main assets of computer information systems.

8. Each spreadsheet report usually contains _____ that identify the organization, purpose, and time period covered.

a. cells

b. columns

c. labels

d. heading entries

◊ ◊ ◊ ◊ ◊ ◊ ◊ ◊ ◊ ◊ ◊ ◊ ◊ ◊ ◊ ◊ ◊ ◊ ◊

d. heading entries. Headings are vital for information users.

9. With spreadsheet programs, function and option selections are made through a _____ .
a. menu screen
b. menu bar
c. prompt screen
d. text window

◊ ◊ ◊ ◊ ◊ ◊ ◊ ◊ ◊ ◊ ◊ ◊ ◊ ◊ ◊ ◊ ◊ ◊ ◊

b. menu bar. A menu bar is a horizontal list.

10. Electronic spreadsheets have given rise to a planning technique called _____ .
a. "What if?" simulation
b. information simulation
c. economic simulation
d. market simulation

◊ ◊ ◊ ◊ ◊ ◊ ◊ ◊ ◊ ◊ ◊ ◊ ◊ ◊ ◊ ◊ ◊ ◊ ◊

a. "What if?" simulation. Spreadsheet simulations enable managers to preview results of multiple decision alternatives.

TRUE/FALSE

DIRECTIONS: *Read each question carefully, then circle either T or F to correctly answer each question.*

1. T F Unlike text files, data items tend to follow uniform structures.

2. T F One drawback to using microcomputers for word processing is the high cost of diskette storage.

3. T F Word processing files are stored, in almost every case, on floppy or hard disks.

4. T F Some word processing packages save the active document when the user presses the F10 function key.

5. T F File managers are capable of interrelating the content of multiple files.

6.   T   F   Relational databases are the most common file handling tools for management applications.

7.   T   F   Most DBMS packages are menu driven.

8.   T   F   Spreadsheets generated manually are easier to change and correct than spreadsheet software computer displays.

9.   T   F   Spreadsheet application packages are credited as the main force for placing microcomputers on the desks of managers and executives.

10.   T   F   A computer can handle data much more rapidly than a communication channel.

MATCHING

DIRECTIONS: *Read each question carefully. Choose the correct answer from the list below and write the letter of the answer in the space provided.*

a.   default   f.   submenu
b.   proofreading   g.   search and replace
c.   formula   h.   prompt screen
d.   bottom line   i.   function keys
e.   diskette   j.   modems

1.   Microcomputers have proven ideal tools for word processing because of the flexibility and low cost of _____ storage.

2.   Command-type programs were replaced rapidly by menu-driven systems following introduction of microcomputers with _____ during the early 1980s.

3.   A _____ is a secondary selection list accessed through choice of an option on a main menu.

4.   A _____ is a display in which the user enters operational specifications for a program.

5.   The detailed checking of a text document to identify keyboarding errors is known as _____ .

6.   The ability of a computer to find strings of characters in text and to replace one designated string with another is known as _____ .

7.   _____ settings are document specifications and format settings built into programs that are applied unless varied by the user.

8.   The _____ entry on a spreadsheet budget, derived by subtracting the total expenses from the total income, indicates projected profit or loss for a given period.

9.   A _____ is an instruction that causes spreadsheet software to perform calculations upon values in cells to derive figures for totals or projections.

10.   A data communication software package is the medium for creating the signals sent and received through _____ .

SHORT ANSWER

DIRECTIONS: Read each question carefully. Answer each question using three or four complete sentences.

1.   What are some of the applications for word processing software in business?

2.   What disadvantages are associated with command-driven systems?

3.   What is the purpose of the "word wrap" feature of a word-processing computer?

4.   What operations do the PgUp and PgDn keys perform?

5.   What is the "strikeover" function of a word processing computer?

6.   What is the "search and replace" capability?

7. What does "WYSIWYG" stand for? What is meant by this term?

8. What advantages does spreadsheet software provide over manual methods for preparation of budgets and spreadsheet reports?

9. How does a user change the column width on a spreadsheet document?

10. What are "buffers?" How do they assist in data communication?

ANSWER KEY

True/False

1. T   3. T   5. F   7. T   9. T

Matching

1. e   3. f   5. b   7. a   9. c

Short Answer Suggested Responses

Your answers for the odd questions should contain most of the information below.

1.   The main application for word processing software is business correspondence. Other applications in business include the production of text documents such as price quotations (bids), proposals, and legal documents.

3.   On a word processing computer, the system uses its word wrap feature to start new lines automatically. The computer senses entry of a word that is too long to fit on the line of text that is currently being entered. On recognizing this, the computer automatically moves the word that will not fit to the beginning of the next line. Therefore, it is not necessary to press the return key at the end of each line, as is required on a typewriter. Return entries are needed only at the ends of paragraphs. This can result in faster typing speeds than with traditional typewriters.

5.   When the cursor is positioned at a character entry on the screen, any character key you strike will replace the existing entry. Thus, the user can correct typographical errors simply by striking over the existing entries.

7.   WYSIWYG is an abbreviation for "What you see is what you get." WYSIWYG refers to a screen formatting capability that allows the user to preview, on the display screen, exactly what a document will look like when it is printed.

9.   To change the column width on a spreadsheet, the user chooses the top line in any column as the active cell. The display indicates the number of character spaces currently in the column and prompts for entry of a new value. For example, to change the column width from a default setting of 10 to a setting of 20, the user would enter the number 20 at the prompt and press the RETURN key.

Chapter 8
Integrated Software,
Graphics, and Desktop Publishing

SUMMARY

Integrated software, graphics, and desktop publishing applications require massive memory and storage capacities. The development of these applications could not occur until capabilities for massive storage and high-speed processing became available. Graphics files, for example, occupy at least 10 times more space per page than text or data files.

Storage capacities have increased continually. The first micro-computers had primary storage capacities of 16,000 to 32,000 bytes. At present, computers are available with 4 megabytes of primary storage and hard disk drives with capacities between 40 and 300 megabytes.

Integrated software refers to sets of programs that make it possible to mix processing and outputs from different, ordinarily incompatible packages. For example, text documents can include data tables created under spreadsheet or database packages. Under some integrated software programs, a common group of commands can be used to control access to files and processing routines for multiple application packages.

Two separate approaches—horizontal integration and vertical integration—can be used to implement software integration. "Horizontal integration" describes the combining of application packages. This type of software tool combines a number of normally independent packages for coordinated use. Existing horizontal integration packages provide rapid access to such applications as word processing, data management, spreadsheet, and graphics. Further, the user can combine elements of outputs from two or more packages into a single document or display.

A "vertical integration" software package combines features that enhance the capabilities of a single package. A word processing program that contains features such as spell checking, a dictionary, or a the-saurus is considered a vertically integrated package.

Window-type software implements horizontal integration. Access to multiple applications is controlled through displays that present menus for the accessible packages. Other integration programs incorporate two or more applications within the same package. These programs permit the exchange of file content between applications.

Graphics software programs adapt computers for development of images. In business, computer graphics can be used to produce graphs and charts for illustrated reports. Presentation graphics encompasses any pictorial materials used at meetings or other gatherings. Visual representations of the ideas being represented can render the information clearer to the audience. Graphics software also is used to assist in product design and development.

A graphics image is formed by segmenting the screen into thousands of individual row and column positions. These positions are called picture elements or "pixels," each of which represents a tiny spot on the computer screen. Each pixel can be addressed, or located, by using a set of binary codes that indicate the pixel's horizontal and vertical positions. This approach to forming images is called "bit mapping." To produce graphics, a special circuit card must be included in the computer's processor. This "graphics card" works as a co-processor to handle data and generate outputs. In addition, massive primary- and secondary-storage capacities are needed to support graphics processing. For example, a page of bit-mapped graphics will require between 35,000 and 40,000 bytes of storage as compared with less than 2,000 for text.

The two general methods used to create graphics are "direct bit mapping" and "vector graphics." Direct bit mapping applies user-controlled software to examine, review, and modify the pixel content of an image. Pixel images are created with "paint" software or through electronic input devices. "Vector graphics" is a technique for drawing lines and shapes on computers. Vector graphics enable the user to generate images— such as pie charts, bar charts, and line graphs— to represent spreadsheet data.

Some applications require the production of full-color graphics. Full-color graphics can be produced through use of a special color graphics card and special software that responds to input instructions that contain color values. Applications for which color graphics often are necessary include slide and video presentations at sales meetings. Color graphics also are used in education, entertainment, advertising, science, and engineering.

Under desktop publishing methods, computers are able to set type and prepare illustrations. Desktop publishing uses special software to convert text prepared under word processing programs into typeset fonts. The type is combined with computer-generated illustrations to produce finished pages. Like computer graphics, desktop publishing requires a microcomputer equipped with a graphics card and large amounts of both primary and secondary storage. In addition, a desktop publishing system needs a file-management program to store and access large numbers of files and a full set of graphics software with both draw and paint capabilities.

An important software tool required by a desktop publishing system is a page-makeup application package. Page-makeup software provides the capability to create and assemble finished publication pages. An operator works from a preliminary design or sketch, known as a "dummy," to set up page layout displays on the computer screen.

Generally, any illustrations are positioned on the pages first. Next, the type is flowed into place at designated points on each page.

The finished pages usually are produced with laser printers or typesetting machines that can generate high-quality, production-ready outputs. The most common standard for laser printers involves outputs at 300 dpi (dots per inch), however, improved laser printers are becoming available that can reproduce images at 600 and 1,000 dpi. The most commonly used typesetting machine generates outputs either at 1,270 or 2,540 dpi. Special software may be needed to convert the dots-per-inch values of the screen image to higher densities for output processing.

Although desktop publishing tends to be sold as a simple, user-friendly process, it is far more complex than other office-type applications of microcomputers. In addition to the special equipment and software requirements, the user will need months of training and practice before attaining a level of practical efficiency. Once mastered, however, desktop publishing can provide great advantages in speed, economy, and quality. Virtually any publication that goes into print can benefit from use of desktop-publishing techniques. Popular applications include marketing support documents, financial information reports, and newsletters. In some instances, desktop publishing methods also can be applied to the production of larger publications, such as magazines, newspapers, and books.

STRUCTURED LEARNING

DIRECTIONS: *First, use a blank sheet of paper to cover the answer, without reading it. Then read the question carefully and write the letter of the correct answer in the space provided. Uncover the answer to see if you chose the correct response.*

1.   Software integration is implemented through two separate approaches known as _____ .
a.   internal and external integration
b.   word processing and graphics integration
c.   horizontal and vertical integration
d.   desktop and clipboard integration

◊ ◊ ◊ ◊ ◊ ◊ ◊ ◊ ◊ ◊ ◊ ◊ ◊ ◊ ◊ ◊ ◊ ◊

   c.   horizontal and vertical integration. Horizontal methods combine output from multiple applications. Vertical methods expand functions of established applications.

2.   Software packages that enable the user to prepare business transaction documents and to generate financial statements through integrated use of the same data files are known as _____ .
a.   integrated accounting systems
b.   business transaction packages

c.   personal accounting programs
d.   professional financial applications

◊ ◊ ◊ ◊ ◊ ◊ ◊ ◊ ◊ ◊ ◊ ◊ ◊ ◊ ◊ ◊ ◊ ◊ ◊

   a.   integrated accounting systems. These systems grow by adding
         files and applications to a database.

3.   A graphics image is formed by segmenting the screen into thousands
       of individual row and column positions. These positions are called
       _____ .
a.   grains
b.   pixels
c.   elements
d.   points

◊ ◊ ◊ ◊ ◊ ◊ ◊ ◊ ◊ ◊ ◊ ◊ ◊ ◊ ◊ ◊ ◊ ◊ ◊

   b.   pixels or "picture elements." Your TV set presents pixelated
         images.

4.   Because vector graphics techniques generate lines, the results are
       known as _____ art.
a.   tone
b.   bit
c.   mathematical
d.   line

◊ ◊ ◊ ◊ ◊ ◊ ◊ ◊ ◊ ◊ ◊ ◊ ◊ ◊ ◊ ◊ ◊ ◊ ◊

   d.   line. The term "line drawing" also applies.

5.   For each page of graphics material, storage requirements are ap-
       proximately _____ times as great as for text or data.
a.   two to three
b.   five to 10
c.   10 to 20
d.   30 to 40

◊ ◊ ◊ ◊ ◊ ◊ ◊ ◊ ◊ ◊ ◊ ◊ ◊ ◊ ◊ ◊ ◊ ◊ ◊

   c.   10 to 20. Graphics images have to be detailed from pixels.
         Character sets are built into system software.

6. Two general methods are available to create graphics: vector graphics and _____ .

a. window-type software
b. direct bit mapping
c. spreadsheet packages
d. page-makeup software

◊ ◊ ◊ ◊ ◊ ◊ ◊ ◊ ◊ ◊ ◊ ◊ ◊ ◊ ◊ ◊ ◊ ◊ ◊

   b. direct bit mapping. Direct bit mapping uses more memory and storage.

7. Changing effects in a human body or in a device under stress can be highlighted through use of _____ .

a. color graphics
b. bar charts
c. line graphs
d. tone values

◊ ◊ ◊ ◊ ◊ ◊ ◊ ◊ ◊ ◊ ◊ ◊ ◊ ◊ ◊ ◊ ◊ ◊ ◊

   a. color graphics. Medical and safety applications are growing in importance.

8. Spacing characters on a line so that both the left and right margins of a column of text are aligned evenly is known as _____ .

a. coordination
b. justification
c. symmetry
d. text adjustment

◊ ◊ ◊ ◊ ◊ ◊ ◊ ◊ ◊ ◊ ◊ ◊ ◊ ◊ ◊ ◊ ◊ ◊ ◊

   b. justification. Justification uses special mathematical computations for horizontal spacing and special hyphenation software that includes a dictionary.

9. Typesetting involves the formatting of text into specific sets of characters, called _____, that are of publication quality.
a. pixels
b. dots
c. fonts
d. vectors

◊ ◊ ◊ ◊ ◊ ◊ ◊ ◊ ◊ ◊ ◊ ◊ ◊ ◊ ◊ ◊ ◊

   c. fonts. Font selection is critical to the appearance of publications.

10. _____ software provides the capability to create and assemble finished publication pages.
a. Drawing
b. Color graphics
c. Paint
d. Page-makeup

◊ ◊ ◊ ◊ ◊ ◊ ◊ ◊ ◊ ◊ ◊ ◊ ◊ ◊ ◊ ◊ ◊

   d. Page makeup. Use of page-makeup software calls for extensive training for experienced people.

TRUE/FALSE

DIRECTIONS: *Read each question carefully, then circle either T or F to correctly answer each question.*

1. T F Computer storage capacities have decreased while hardware costs have increased.

2. T F Under integrated software programs, file content from multiple applications can be consolidated into the same output documents.

3. T F Window-type software packages require more operator training than is needed for the use of a single package.

4. T F A word-processing program with a dictionary and spell-checking capability is an example of horizontal integration.

5. T F Producing graphics through the use of computer tools is more difficult and costly than manual methods.

6.   T   F   A pie chart presents information on trends over time periods as positions on a graph, traced by "trend lines."

7.   T   F   On a display screen, there are many more pixels than characters of text.

8.   T   F   Images created with paint software do not have tone values.

9.   T   F   Vector graphics can be used to produce lines and curves that indicate patient heart rates on printed outputs called electrocardiograms.

10.   T   F   Desktop publishing is an ideal method for producing newsletters.

MATCHING

DIRECTIONS: *Read each question carefully. Choose the correct answer from the list below and write the letter of the answer in the space provided.*

a.   dots-per-inch (dpi)
b.   full-color graphics
c.   paint
d.   graphics card
e.   product development

f.   histogram
g.   window-type
h.   bit mapping
i.   graphics aids
j.   general ledger

1.   Graphics capabilities are implemented through an imaging technique known as _____ .

2.   A _____ software package provides a mechanism for interaction and linkage between independent programs such as word processors, database management systems, and spreadsheets.

3.   Integrated accounting systems can be used to generate _____ reports that detail the financial status and condition of a business on given dates.

4.   Slides, video images, and printed notes or illustrations used at meetings are examples of _____ .

5.   A bar chart, or _____ , represents values as a series of lines (or bars) of varying lengths.

6.   As an early stage in the process of _____ , it is necessary to prepare pictures of the item under development.

7. To produce graphics, a _____ must be included in the computer's processor.

8. Pixel images are created with _____ software or through electronic input devices.

9. Generating _____ is accomplished through a process that is similar to the imaging of color television pictures.

10. In general, the greater the _____ density, the better the quality of the printed output.

SHORT ANSWER

DIRECTIONS: *Read each question carefully. Answer each question using three or four complete sentences.*

1. What capabilities are made possible through the use of integrated software?

2. What advantages are provided by window-type software?

3.   Name some of the features that vertical integration can combine with word-processing programs.

4.   What purpose do presentation graphics serve?

5.   What are some of the common applications of vector graphics in business?

6.   How does the entertainment industry use color graphics?

7. What are the hardware and software requirements of a desktop-publishing system?

8. Why is a file-management program a critical component of a desktop-publishing system?

9. How does typeset print differ from "typewriter-quality" print?

10. How are desktop publishing techniques used for marketing support applications?

ANSWER KEY
True/False

1. F   3. T   5. F   7. T   9. T

Matching

1. h   3. j   5. f   7. d   9. b

Short Answer Suggested Responses

Your answers for the odd questions should contain most of the information below.

1. Capabilities made possible through use of integrated software include the following: a computer can access and process a number of different applications that normally cannot be used at the same time; file content from multiple applications can be consolidated into the same output documents; and a common group of commands can be used to control access to files and processing routines for multiple application packages.

3. Vertical integration can enhance the capabilities of a word-processing program with such features as spell checking, a dictionary, or a thesaurus.

5. Common uses of vector graphics in business are for charts and diagrams. Also, the graphics generated by spreadsheet software—pie charts, bar charts, and line graphs—are produced through vector graphics methods.

7. A desktop publishing system requires a microcomputer equipped with a graphics card, large amounts of both primary and secondary storage, an output capability that produces reproduction-quality end products, a file management program, a full set of graphics software with both draw and paint capabilities, a program with both word processing and typesetting capabilities, and a page-makeup application package.

9. Typesetting involves the formatting of text into specific sets of characters, called "fonts," that are of publication quality. When a document is typeset, each character within a line of text occupies a different width, making for an orderly, attractive appearance. Typeset text usually is justified. The most commonly used typesetting machine generates outputs either at 1,270 or 2,540 dpi. Typewriter-quality print generally refers to character sets used for correspondence.

Chapter 9

The Automated Office

SUMMARY

Innovations in communications, information storage and retrieval, and software are leading to the computerization of today's business offices. Today, the working environment of clerical and administrative personnel is known as the "electronic office." Almost every office function, including typing, filing, and communication, can be automated.

Most U.S. companies use some form of word processing, the most widely adopted office automation. Clerical personnel can increase their productivity by 25 to 200 percent by using word processing capabilities. Even more important, executive efficiency can be increased by as much as 5 to 10 percent.

Office automation can use local area networks. LAN users share files, devices, and programs. Problems of compatibility and cost effectiveness are being overcome rapidly so that more and more organizations are implementing LANs.

Today's office telephone may be a computer peripheral. Information can be transmitted through telephones linked to computers. Within some systems, telephone calls can include data displays between computer systems. Facsimile (fax) devices use telephone lines to transmit images of documents.

Office efficiency also is being increased through the use of electronic mail, the process of transmitting text at high speeds over telecommunication facilities. Electronic mail relies on a combination of data transmission, storage, and retrieval capabilities for the exchange of messages among users. These messages can involve text, images, or voice recordings. "Voice store and forward" service (voice mail) produces a recorded audio message instead of hard copy.

Electronic mail capabilities are being expanded in many companies through use of "electronic calendaring." Under control of special software, key managers and other personnel record their appointments, meetings, and travel plans through entries in screens that resemble appointment calendars. Electronic calendaring can facilitate appointment scheduling while electronic mail can be used to deliver information.

The technologies for image reproduction and computing are being merged in systems that reproduce actual documents within computer files. Through an application known as "image processing," source documents are captured graphically through use of video cameras or scanners. The images are recorded in magnetic or laser disk devices. Application software can retrieve and reproduce the images through use of laser printers or other xerographic devices.

In most large organizations, managers often spend the majority of their time in meetings. When meetings involve travel, costs of air fare and accommodations can be major. Telecommunication and computer capabilities can save time and money through teleconferencing, video-conferencing, and computer conferencing.

Teleconferencing brings participants in a meeting together through use of telephone voice channels. One method of teleconferencing, the "conference call," connects multiple parties for joint conversations. This approach enables managers and executives to conduct business over the telephone as though they were in the same room. An "audio conference" is a type of conference call in which the participants gather in local conference rooms equipped to amplify telephone conversations through speakers.

Videoconferencing is a teleconferencing method involving two or more sites linked by video and audio systems. Under one approach, participants can communicate through one-way video and two-way audio transmission. A more sophisticated arrangement involves full, two-way video coverage from all locations.

A computer conference is a meeting in which each participant works at a microcomputer or a terminal linked to a large computer. One person is designated as the "facilitator," or coordinator. This individual is responsible for handling advance preparations, controlling the agenda, and reviewing contributions by participants. At the start of the meeting, the facilitor poses a question or states a problem to all participants. The participants provide responses through entries on their keyboard. This approach can save time because, unlike in-person meetings where only one person may speak at a time, all participants in a computer conference can contribute at the same time.

Computer capabilities are opening some options for alternative work patterns, including flex time, satellite offices, and telecommuting. "Flex time" plans allow employees to vary their work schedules based on personal need and convenience. Information, instructions, and documents are transmitted through computer-stored files. "Satellite offices," work facilities set up in suburban locations, eliminate some of the problems involved in commuting to downtown offices. Information and work assignments are exchanged through data-communication networks. "Telecommuting" enables people to work away from the office, through the use of computer hookups. While these alternatives have become technically feasible, it is likely that human factors—such as the need for personal contact and social interaction—will limit their use.

Ergonomics is the science of studying and changing the work environment to suit the worker. Ergonomists working in the computer industry are designing computers and keyboards that are easier to use. Manufacturers of office furniture are designing chairs to help combat lower back pain. Of primary concern to ergonomists is the health of the worker who spends eight hours a day in front of a computer monitor. Video display terminal operators commonly complain of eye strain, aches and pains, excessive fatigue, and stress. While some of these problems can be alleviated by improving environmental conditions and machine design, experts recommend that terminal operators take regular rest periods. Some European countries and some local governments in the United States have passed legislation covering special work rules for VDT operators.

STRUCTURED LEARNING

DIRECTIONS: *First, use a blank sheet of paper to cover the answer, without reading it. Then read the question carefully and write the letter of the correct answer in the space provided. Uncover the answer to see if you chose the correct response.*

1. Word processing, electronic mail, information retrieval, and teleconferencing are specific _____ applications.
   a. electronic spreadsheet
   b. office automation
   c. computer conferencing
   d. local area network

◊ ◊ ◊ ◊ ◊ ◊ ◊ ◊ ◊ ◊ ◊ ◊ ◊ ◊ ◊ ◊ ◊ ◊ ◊

   b.   office automation. This term applies to the processes that integrate computer and communication technology with traditional office procedures.

2. The most widely used type of office automation technology is _____ .
   a. word processing
   b. electronic mail
   c. voice message systems
   d. teleconferencing

◊ ◊ ◊ ◊ ◊ ◊ ◊ ◊ ◊ ◊ ◊ ◊ ◊ ◊ ◊ ◊ ◊ ◊ ◊

   a.   word processing. Approximately 80 percent of U.S. companies employ some form of word processing.

3. The process of transmitting text very quickly over telecommunications equipment is known as _____ .
   a. word processing
   b. voice mail
   c. teleconferencing
   d. electronic mail

◊ ◊ ◊ ◊ ◊ ◊ ◊ ◊ ◊ ◊ ◊ ◊ ◊ ◊ ◊ ◊ ◊ ◊ ◊

    d.   electronic mail. The purpose is to eliminate costs and delays of traditional mail and enable senders and receivers of messages to control transmission and delivery.

4. It is estimated that clerical personnel can increase their productivity by _____ percent if word processing capabilities are included in their workstations.
a. 5 to 10
b. 10 to 15
c. 15 to 25
d. 25 to 200

◊ ◊ ◊ ◊ ◊ ◊ ◊ ◊ ◊ ◊ ◊ ◊ ◊ ◊ ◊ ◊ ◊ ◊ ◊

    d.   25 to 200. Word processing also can increase executive efficiency by as much as 5 to 10 percent, a significant increase considering their level of responsibility.

5. _____ devices provide capabilities for the transmission and reproduction of paper documents through use of telecommunication channels.
a. Slow-scan video
b. Facsimile (fax)
c. Electronic calendaring
d. Teleconferencing

◊ ◊ ◊ ◊ ◊ ◊ ◊ ◊ ◊ ◊ ◊ ◊ ◊ ◊ ◊ ◊ ◊ ◊ ◊

    b.   Facsimile. Facsimile devices use telephone lines to transmit and receive images of documents.

6. A form of teleconferencing in which two or more sites are linked by video and audio systems is known as _____ .
a. electronic calendaring
b. telecommuting
c. videoconferencing
d. image processing

◊ ◊ ◊ ◊ ◊ ◊ ◊ ◊ ◊ ◊ ◊ ◊ ◊ ◊ ◊ ◊ ◊ ◊ ◊

    c.   videoconferencing. Participants can view documents or products on video screens.

7.   _____ are facilities set up in suburban locations near to where workers reside.
a.   Satellite offices
b.   Workstations
c.   Home offices
d.   Civic centers

◊ ◊ ◊ ◊ ◊ ◊ ◊ ◊ ◊ ◊ ◊ ◊ ◊ ◊ ◊ ◊ ◊ ◊ ◊

a.   Satellite offices. Suburban locations can, in many instances, eliminate commuting problems for workers and allow businesses to rent space at lower costs.

8.   _____ allows employees to work at home rather than at an office.
a.   Teleconferencing
b.   Ergonomics
c.   Image processing
d.   Telecommuting

◊ ◊ ◊ ◊ ◊ ◊ ◊ ◊ ◊ ◊ ◊ ◊ ◊ ◊ ◊ ◊ ◊ ◊ ◊

d.   Telecommuting. Telecommuting enables individuals who have offices or work facilities at home to stay in touch with the office through computer terminals.

9.   The science of adapting work environments to suit the worker is known as _____ .
a.   environmental adaption
b.   office automation
c.   ergonomics
d.   aerodynamics

◊ ◊ ◊ ◊ ◊ ◊ ◊ ◊ ◊ ◊ ◊ ◊ ◊ ◊ ◊ ◊ ◊ ◊ ◊

c.   ergonomics. Ergonomics strives to increase employee productivity by making the work environment more comfortable.

10. Which of the following is *not* a method that ergonomists are using to improve workers' environments? _____ .
a.   redesigning VDT screens
b.   redesigning office furniture
c.   redesigning computer software
d.   pushing for legislation to protect VDT operators

◊ ◊ ◊ ◊ ◊ ◊ ◊ ◊ ◊ ◊ ◊ ◊ ◊ ◊ ◊ ◊ ◊ ◊ ◊

c.   redesigning computer software. Ergonomics is concerned with the work environment rather than the computer applications.

TRUE/FALSE

DIRECTIONS: *Read each question carefully, then circle either T or F to correctly answer each question.*

1. T F Office automation refers to the linking of CPUs and terminals by a communication system within a limited area, such as a building or complex of buildings.

2. T F Local area networks provide a form of teleconferencing.

3. T F Workstations generally are equipped with a microcomputer that has data communications capabilities.

4. T F An Information Resources Manager is responsible for an organization's computing and telecommunication facilities.

5. T F Videoconferencing has been accepted universally among corporations as an effective management tool.

6. T F An advantage of a computer conference is that all participants can be entering their contributions at the same time.

7. T F Telecommuting enables managers or executives who travel extensively to work at home part of the time to compensate for time spent away from home and families.

8. T F Under flex-time arrangements, two part-time employees can share one job.

9. T F Ergonomists are concerned primarily with the health and comfort of managers in supervisory positions.

10. T F In Sweden, the government has recommended that VDT workers spend no more than four hours a day at a terminal.

MATCHING

DIRECTIONS: *Read each question carefully. Choose the correct answer from the list below and write the letter of the answer in the space provided.*

a. teleconferencing   f. voice mail
b. duplication   g. image processing
c. word processing   h. flex time
d. electronic mail   i. groupware
e. facilitator   j. electronic calendaring

1. Local area networks eliminate the _____ of equipment, databases, and actions.

2. The most widely adopted office automation technology is _____ .

3. A company can save both time and money using _____ while ensuring that information arrives on time at its destination.

4. A computer-based message transmission system that utilizes a recorded message rather than hard copy is _____ .

5. Businesses can save time and travel expense through _____ .

6. During a computer conference, the _____ poses a question or states a problem to the participants, who respond through entries on their keyboards.

7. Computer conferencing is being supported, within many organizations, by a recently introduced kind of application software, known as _____ .

8. A working arrangement which allows employees to set work schedules based on personal needs and convenience—within frameworks established by their employers—is called _____ .

9. _____ capabilities permit managers and other personnel to record and display their appointment schedules through use of special software.

10. _____ is an application that scans images through video techniques, records images in computer storage, and produces graphic outputs.

SHORT ANSWER

DIRECTIONS: *Read each question carefully. Answer each question using three or four complete sentences.*

1. What are LANs, and what are the advantages companies can obtain through their use?

2.   What is a workstation? What basic components make up a work-
      station?

3.   How do facsimile devices transmit images of documents?

4.   What is slow-scan video?

5.   What is the main drawback to using electronic meeting methods?

6.   Why aren't most large corporations making use of videoconferenc-
      ing?

7.   What is the main obstacle to implementation of electronic mail techniques?

8.   How have ergonomists improved the microcomputer to better suit its users over the past decade?

9.   Which workers in the computer field are attracting special attention from ergonomists?

10.   What could legislation do to improve conditions for VDT operators?

ANSWER KEY

True/False

1. F	3. T	5. F	7. T	9. F

Matching

1. b	3. d	5. a	7. i	9. j

Short Answer Suggested Responses

Your answers for the odd questions should contain most of the information below.

1. LANs are local area networks, a group of linked CPUs and terminals in a well-defined area. They allow the integration of office automation capabilities. LANs allow users to share files, devices, and programs, and they eliminate unnecessary duplication of equipment, databases, and actions.

3. Facsimile devices transit images of documents through telephone lines. At the sending end, a document is placed in a feeding unit that includes a scanner. The light-sensing scanner transmits digital signals to a receiving fax machine, where the document is reproduced.

5. Electronic meeting methods reduce opportunities for personal interaction among skilled people with common interests. Exchanging ideas in person can be important, though the values are intangible.

7. The main obstacle to implementation of electronic mail lies in getting people accustomed to the idea of receiving mail through their computer terminals. People who have electronic mailboxes must check for their messages regularly, just as they do for telephone messages or traditional mail.

9. Ergonomists are concentrating on trying to improve conditions for the VDT operator who has to stare at a monitor screen day after day.

Chapter 10

Computers in Business and Industry

SUMMARY

Computers perform most profitably when they are put to work on large volumes of repetitive tasks. Thus, computers are ideally suited to handle many jobs in business and industry.

To reduce demands for the handling of paper documents, banks utilize computer applications that process financial transactions through electronic communication between computers. This approach is known as electronic funds transfer (ETF). Automatic teller machines are a form of EFT, enabling bank customers to process transactions on their own, at any time. Home banking also is possible with EFT. Through a microcomputer and a modem, or just a touch-tone telephone, a customer can perform transactions through entries on a microcomputer keyboard or the keypad of a telephone. Other forms of EFT include the smart card, a microchip embedded in a thin plastic card that allows the user to make purchases on a debit basis, and point-of-sale terminals, designed to authorize and complete credit card transactions, transferring funds instantly from the customer's account to the merchant's.

Insurance companies, securities dealers, and companies that do business through customer reservations also make use of computer capabilities to handle large volumes of paperwork. Computers enable insurance agents to provide on-line responses to applications for coverage and to assist in the processing of claims. The New York Stock Exchange and the major securities trading facilities use networks of computers to keep pace with increasingly larger transaction volumes. All major airlines, hotels, car-rental companies, theaters, and sports stadiums use database systems for customer reservations. Reservation systems have become a necessity for these types of businesses.

Microcomputers have become essential to management within many organizations. Word processors and electronic spreadsheet programs are two of the applications most frequently used by managers to save time and make tasks easier. In particular, managers with budget-preparation responsibilities save time and increase productivity with electronic spreadsheet software. Many managers report a pattern of increasing reliance on microcomputers and many purchase machines for home use. These individuals sometimes spend a substantial portion of their time working at home.

Because computers make it so easy to generate and retrieve information, many managers suffer from information overload. Finding the right data can be difficult for managers who are flooded with paperwork. Graphics displays help to reduce the information overload and facilitate decision making. Comparisons, relationships, trends, and essential points can be spotted through use of tools such as graphics outputs from spreadsheet programs.

Today, the majority of companies are information-dependent. Many companies have instituted organizational changes that consolidate responsibilities for information management under a top-level individual, often called the Information Resources Manager (IRM). The responsibilities of an IRM include overseeing such functions as computer-supported administration, telecommunications, data processing, systems development, and database management.

"Decision support system" software and "artificial intelligence" software can assist managers in decision making. Decision support system software assembles and processes data to project outcomes of decision alternatives. Based on the resulting information, managers can choose the best solution or course of action. Artificial intelligence software enables a decision maker to assemble sets of facts and rules as a basis for selecting decision alternatives or trouble shooting. At present, medical diagnosis is the most widely used application of artificial intelligence.

In the business world, microcomputers also are used to record and facilitate sales, update inventories, and make projections on expected sales. Insurance agents often use portable microcomputers in the field to supply clients with the policy information needed to make a sale. Computers also support at-home shopping. Consumers interact with special TV broadcasts carried over cable networks. Viewers order items by making entries on special devices linked to the cable network or by telephoning specified numbers.

Computers are being used by marketing service organizations to test new products and to test markets for products. Computer simulations can project product sales in an area.

Many computer programs help to make industry more efficient. Materials requirement planning (MRP) can be used to control inventory. Computer-aided design (CAD) utilizes graphics to help in designing, drafting, and analyzing products. Computer-aided manufacturing (CAM) simulates the manufacturing process so that problems in production can be remedied before they actually arise. Virtually every area of manufacturing has incorporated CAD/CAM techniques. The aerospace and automotive industries have been innovators in CAD/CAM. Computer-integrated manufacturing (CIM) ties CAD and CAM together.

Robotics refers to the use of robots in production or service applications. First-generation robots have mechanical dexterity, but no external senses. Second-generation robots possess crude tactile and visual senses. Robots can be used in hazardous positions in industry and even in the military. Bin-picking robots use a complex series of movements to find and sort objects from a collection of many kinds of items.

Robots can reduce labor costs. They also are easier to manage than human workers. There also can be disadvantages to the use of robots. For example, robots can be damaged by surges of electricity or cause injury to humans in the workplace. Because robots are incapable of recognizing errors and exercising judgment, they may contribute to the production of faulty goods.

Manufacturing and process industries use computers to monitor quality control. One manufacturing application is nondestructive testing (NDT). In NDT, microcomputers are combined with X-rays, high-frequency sound waves, and/or laser beams to inspect the interiors of products. This process uncovers interior flaws without damaging the products. Statistical quality control involves the use of a computer to monitor trends in conditions or tolerances for continuous operations or processes so that corrective action can be taken before problems arise. Examples of applications include petroleum refining, food processing, and metalworking operations.

STRUCTURED LEARNING

DIRECTIONS: First, use a blank sheet of paper to cover the answer, without reading it. Then read the question carefully and write the letter of the correct answer in the space provided. Uncover the answer to see if you chose the correct response.

1.   Unattended remote devices that bank customers use to withdraw or deposit funds are called _____ .
   a.   electronic teller devices
   b.   automated teller machines (ATMs)
   c.   telecom bank devices
   d.   funds transfer devices

◊ ◊ ◊ ◊ ◊ ◊ ◊ ◊ ◊ ◊ ◊ ◊ ◊ ◊ ◊ ◊ ◊ ◊

   b.   automated teller machines. ATMs are found outside banks and in supermarkets, airports, college campuses, and shopping malls. The idea is to provide banking convenience.

2.   _____ is a cashless method of managing money in which accounts involved in a transaction are adjusted by electronic communication between computers.
   a.   Electronic funds transfer (EFT)
   b.   Electronic money management
   c.   Computer-assisted management
   d.   Automatic accounting

◊ ◊ ◊ ◊ ◊ ◊ ◊ ◊ ◊ ◊ ◊ ◊ ◊ ◊ ◊ ◊ ◊ ◊

   a. Electronic funds transfer (EFT). Electronic funds transfer involves the transfer of funds from account to account by electronic communication between computers or computer terminals.

3. Managers at every level are coming to depend on _____ like they do their telephones or cars.
a. CAD
b. CAM
c. word processors
d. microcomputers

◊ ◊ ◊ ◊ ◊ ◊ ◊ ◊ ◊ ◊ ◊ ◊ ◊ ◊ ◊ ◊ ◊ ◊

   d. microcomputers. Managers are finding that microcomputers make their work much easier. Word processors and electronic spreadsheets are only two of the applications managers depend upon.

4. _____ percent of management's decisions are based on _____ percent of a company's data.
a. 90/10
b. 80/20
c. 70/30
d. 60/40

◊ ◊ ◊ ◊ ◊ ◊ ◊ ◊ ◊ ◊ ◊ ◊ ◊ ◊ ◊ ◊ ◊ ◊

   b. 80/20. This 20 percent should represent a company's core data.

5. Because of the ease in generating and retrieving information with microcomputers, managers often _____ .
a. suffer from information overload
b. overlook manual alternatives
c. overwork employees
d. overwork themselves

◊ ◊ ◊ ◊ ◊ ◊ ◊ ◊ ◊ ◊ ◊ ◊ ◊ ◊ ◊ ◊ ◊ ◊

   a. suffer from information overload. It is difficult for managers to locate the right data when they are overloaded with paper.

6. Responsibilities for information management may be placed with a top-level individual, often called the _____ .
a. information supervisor
b. director of information
c. information administrator
d. information resources manager

◊ ◊ ◊ ◊ ◊ ◊ ◊ ◊ ◊ ◊ ◊ ◊ ◊ ◊ ◊ ◊ ◊ ◊

   d. information resources manager. Information has value vital to planning and decision making.

7. Marketing service organizations use _____ to test the marketability of products and project sales.
a. simulated test markets
b. projected sales markets
c. materials requirement planning
d. numerical control programs

◊ ◊ ◊ ◊ ◊ ◊ ◊ ◊ ◊ ◊ ◊ ◊ ◊ ◊ ◊ ◊ ◊ ◊

   a. simulated test markets. Simulated test markets have been in use since the mid-1970s. STMs can save millions of dollars in product development.

8. In many companies, _____ controls inventory.
a. CAD
b. CAM
c. MRP
d. CIM

◊ ◊ ◊ ◊ ◊ ◊ ◊ ◊ ◊ ◊ ◊ ◊ ◊ ◊ ◊ ◊ ◊ ◊

   c. MRP. Materials requirement planning (MRP) consists of programs that allow manufacturers to enter projected demands and receive reports listing the manufacturing schedule and the raw materials needed to produce a product.

9. Of the following, which is *not* a type of problem best solved with CAD systems? _____
a. mechanical drafting
b. printed circuit board design
c. scheduling
d. photogrammetry

   c.   scheduling. Three other types of problems CAD systems are particularly well suited to solving are: engineering, architecture, and cartography mapping.

10. X-rays, high-frequency sound waves, and laser beams are used in conjunction with microcomputers to look for internal flaws in products in _____ .

a.   CAD

b.   CAM

c.   CIM

d.   NDT

   d.   NDT. Quality is assured without having to destroy test products.

TRUE/FALSE

DIRECTIONS: *Read each question carefully, then circle either T or F to correctly answer each question.*

1.   T F   When they were introduced, microcomputers faced some deep-seated prejudices among managers.

2.   T F   Managers seem to develop an increasing reliance on computers the more they use them.

3.   T F   Customers who use ATM cards to make retail purchases must keep track of all charges and make monthly payments according to schedules set up by their banks.

4.   T F   In the future, artificial intelligence is expected to play major roles in trouble shooting and/or planning aspects of business management.

5.   T F   Simulated test markets utilize computers to project sales of new products.

6.   T F   The production of very large scale integrated circuits has not been effectively aided by CAD/CAM because of the human element necessary in building the chips.

7.   T F   MRP (materials requirement planning) is a process tying CAD and CAM together, coordinating a manufacturer's operations.

8.   T F   CIM (computer-integrated manufacturing) controls the design and manufacture of a company's products.

9.   T   F   Manufacturers can use robots to perform spot welding and spray painting.

10.   T   F   Nondestructive testing (NDT) uses computer simulations to anticipate problems in production.

MATCHING

DIRECTIONS: *Read each question carefully. Choose the correct answer from the list below and write the letter of the answer in the space provided.*

a. statistical quality control
b. information overload
c. NDT
d. EFT
e. smart card

f. graphics
g. communication
h. CAD/CAM
i. decision support system
j. CIM

1. ATMs are a form of _____ .

2. A(n) _____ functions on a debit basis.

3. Because they facilitate _____ , microcomputers have become essential to management within many organizations.

4. A potential problem for managers using microcomputers is _____ .

5. _____ displays can make information clearer and facilitate decision making.

6. _____ software enables a manager to assemble and process information relevant to a given problem or future opportunity.

7. An engineer can analyze not only products but the manufacturing process as well with _____ .

8. Both the design and manufacture of a company's products can be integrated with _____ .

9. By using _____ methods, inspections can be conducted to locate problems or determine the absence of problems without reducing the value and usability of the products.

10. _____ methods are used to monitor operations in petroleum refining, food processing, and metalworking.

SHORT ANSWER

DIRECTIONS: *Read each question carefully. Answer each question using three or four complete sentences.*

1. How do banks use computers?

2. What are the main advantages of using ATM cards for retail purchases?

3. What two microcomputer applications are used most often by managers?

4. How do computer graphics capabilities aid managers and executives?

5.   How do securities dealers use computer systems to facilitate their operations?

6.   How do computers assist distribution companies in their operations?

7.   How are marketing-service organizations making use of computers?

8.   What is computer-integrated manufacturing (CIM)?

9. How are nondestructive testing methods used to improve airline safety?

10. Why are second-generation robots often called "bin-picking" robots?

ANSWER KEY

True/False

1. T   3. F   5. T   7. F   9. T

Matching

1. d   3. g   5. f   7. h   9. c

Short Answer Suggested Responses

Your answers for the odd questions should contain most of the information below.

1. Banks use computers to facilitate the processing of checks and deposit slips, and to keep up with savings club and investment information. They also use computers to transfer data and funds from bank to bank. Computers support use of ATMS.

3. Word processors and electronic spreadsheets save managers a great deal of time and make many tasks much easier.

5. The major securities trading firms enter buy and sell orders into computer systems. These computers, which are linked directly to

transaction processing computers at the New York Stock Exchange, can execute buy and sell orders in seconds. Computers keep track of and fill all orders automatically, advising the brokers who complete the paperwork later.

7. Marketing-service organizations use computers to test new products and project sales by analyzing the buying patterns of test households. Simulated test markets are growing in popularity as they become more and more accurate. By using these methods, industry can save millions of dollars in research and development on products with inadequate market potential.

9. NDT is used to examine the interior of aircraft engines and to test parts of an airplane's fuselage for metal fatigue.

Chapter 11
Computers in Education

SUMMARY

Computer literacy encompasses a basic understanding of computer terminology, how a computer works, and how people use computers to solve problems. The elements that comprise computer literacy change constantly as the technology develops. In addition, the objectives of computer literacy are different, for example, for a third grader and for a high school student.

Educators are beginning to realize that computers can help them. Applications include opportunities for self-paced student learning, preparation of grade reports, and development of tests and other instructional materials (such as visual aids). However, computers are still not welcomed universally and many teachers need incentives to attend classes, seminars, and workshops on the new technology.

Computer-assisted instruction (CAI) allows students to learn at their own pace and receive immediate feedback following each response they make. Drills, tutorials, simulations, and games are kinds of CAI. Drill-type software is used for factual review of subject material. Tutorials are programs that introduce students to new material and quiz them on their understanding of the information presented. Simulations allow students to use models of real-world events and challenges them to observe, measure, predict, and experiment. Electronic games can help students to develop hand-eye coordination, and logic and problem-solving skills.

Skill-training programs help to prepare students for entry into the job market. Under these programs, students can learn skills such as touch keyboarding (typing), computer drafting, and how to prepare business documents.

Some schools allow students to access information services. Students also can communicate electronically with students at other schools, exchanging games, newsletters, and programs written by students.

Videodiscs can be used with computers to present material to students with motion and sound, as in a movie. Videodisc technology allows students to interact with the program.

Some schools concentrate on programming. There is controversy over which programming language, BASIC or Pascal, is the best beginning language for high school students. BASIC can be used with most microcomputers, and it is easy to learn. However, it can encourage bad programming habits. Pascal, on the other hand, has a widely accepted standard and encourages stuctured programming, but it is harder to learn than BASIC. Another language, Logo, is useful in teaching very young children to program.

Many of the first attempts at computer courses in schools failed. Often, too much of the budget for computer education would be spent on hardware and training, leaving inadequate funds for purchasing software to support the equipment. In some instances, schools lacked personnel with sufficient knowledge to select appropriate software. Often, too, the software itself was poorly designed. Today, software for educational purposes is improving, and awareness of what computer literacy courses require is growing. The South Brunswick, New Jersey school system has developed a model computer literacy program.

Colleges and universities are encouraging students to buy personal computers. Many are requiring that students have them; they arrange for group discounts. Some colleges even include the price of a microcomputer in tuition costs.

Computers have come a long way in schools over the past decade. Formerly looked at strictly as programming or computational tools, computers now fulfill a host of learning applications. Some universities even allow students to earn college credits at home or from other universities via microcomputers and communication links.

STRUCTURED LEARNING

DIRECTIONS: First, use a blank sheet of paper to cover the answer, without reading it. Then read the question carefully and write the letter of the correct answer in the space provided. Uncover the answer to see if you chose the correct response.

1.   Computer literacy refers to _____ .
a.   a general, basic understanding of computers
b.   a basic understanding of programming languages
c.   an extensive understanding of computer hardware
d.   an extensive understanding of programming languages

◊ ◊ ◊ ◊ ◊ ◊ ◊ ◊ ◊ ◊ ◊ ◊ ◊ ◊ ◊ ◊ ◊ ◊ ◊

a.   a general, basic understanding of computers. Computer literacy generally means having a basic understanding of computer terminology, how a computer works, and how to use computers to solve problems.

2. A problem with computer education programs so far lies in the fact that many _____ for one reason or another, have not welcomed computers into education.

a. students
b. parents
c. teachers
d. community citizens

◊ ◊ ◊ ◊ ◊ ◊ ◊ ◊ ◊ ◊ ◊ ◊ ◊ ◊ ◊ ◊ ◊ ◊ ◊

    c.   teachers. Many teachers and administrators are finding the computer technology difficult to learn themselves, so they are reluctant to try teaching it. Others have more philosophical reasons for not approving use of computers in the classroom.

3. The use of computers to instruct students is called _____ .

a. computer literacy
b. computer-assisted instruction
c. computer-aided objectives
d. electronic education

◊ ◊ ◊ ◊ ◊ ◊ ◊ ◊ ◊ ◊ ◊ ◊ ◊ ◊ ◊ ◊ ◊ ◊ ◊

    b.   computer-assisted instruction. CAI is an excellent way to instruct individual students, slow and fast learners, and small groups of students at their own pace.

4. Of the following, which is *not* a kind of CAI? _____

a. drills
b. tutorials
c. summaries
d. games

◊ ◊ ◊ ◊ ◊ ◊ ◊ ◊ ◊ ◊ ◊ ◊ ◊ ◊ ◊ ◊ ◊ ◊ ◊

    c.   summaries. Drills, tutorials, simulations, and games are all kinds of CAI.

5. A technology that combines use of computers with _____ brings lifelike exercises into the classroom.

a. videotape players
b. videodisc players
c. video games
d. hard disk storage devices

◊ ◊ ◊ ◊ ◊ ◊ ◊ ◊ ◊ ◊ ◊ ◊ ◊ ◊ ◊ ◊ ◊ ◊

    b.   videodisc players. Videodisc lessons have sound and visual qualities of film but permit students to interact with the system to ensure that learning takes place.

6.   _____ is a programming language associated with small children, but it is a derivative of LISP, an advanced language used by scientists in artificial intelligence applications.

a.   BASIC
b.   Pascal
c.   COBOL
d.   Logo

◊ ◊ ◊ ◊ ◊ ◊ ◊ ◊ ◊ ◊ ◊ ◊ ◊ ◊ ◊ ◊ ◊ ◊

    d.   Logo. Logo uses turtle graphics and sprites to create graphics displays. Logo is both easy to learn and flexible, rendering it useful for many applications, particularly in education.

7.   When computers first were introduced in schools, educators often neglected to budget enough money for _____ .

a.   hardware
b.   software
c.   training
d.   maintenance

◊ ◊ ◊ ◊ ◊ ◊ ◊ ◊ ◊ ◊ ◊ ◊ ◊ ◊ ◊ ◊ ◊ ◊

    b.   software. Many administrators were lured into a race to get the most advanced technology they could afford without considering the need for good software to support the equipment.

8.   Many computer companies are offering substantial discounts on _____ to students on college campuses.

a.   hardware
b.   software
c.   maintenance
d.   training

◊ ◊ ◊ ◊ ◊ ◊ ◊ ◊ ◊ ◊ ◊ ◊ ◊ ◊ ◊ ◊ ◊ ◊

    a.   hardware. Apple, IBM, Digital Equipment Corporation (DEC), and Zenith are among the companies offering hardware discounts to college students.

9. Many people have expressed concern that the proliferation of microcomputers on campus might harm students' _____ .
a. reasoning abilities
b. socialization processes
c. learning skills
d. imaginations

◊ ◊ ◊ ◊ ◊ ◊ ◊ ◊ ◊ ◊ ◊ ◊ ◊ ◊ ◊ ◊ ◊ ◊

    b.   socialization processes. Many people thought that students would lock themselves up in their rooms with their computers, becoming hermits. Students seem to be adjusting very well, however, to working and living with computers.

10. _____ is an easy-to-learn programming language, but it encourages poor programming habits.
a. Logo
b. COBOL
c. Pascal
d. BASIC

◊ ◊ ◊ ◊ ◊ ◊ ◊ ◊ ◊ ◊ ◊ ◊ ◊ ◊ ◊ ◊ ◊ ◊

    d.   BASIC. BASIC encourages the use of GOTO statements; these statements cause loops in programs, making the programs difficult for anyone but the original programmer to modify.

TRUE/FALSE

DIRECTIONS: *Read each question carefully, then circle either T or F to correctly answer each question.*

1. T F   Computer literacy refers to the ability to communicate with computer hardware via an assortment of programming languages.

2. T   F   Teachers seem to have almost universally hailed the computer as the most important educational advancement of the decade.

3. T   F   Teachers all over the country are attending classes, seminars, and workshops to become computer literate themselves.

4. T   F   Computer literacy programs are much easier to maintain now than they were a few years ago because the technology has leveled out and advances are not occurring as quickly.

5. T   F   Drills, tutorials, simulations, and games are all kinds of computer-aided design (CAD).

6. T   F   CAI programs provide students with a patient teacher.

7. T   F   Pascal is frequently associated with small children, but it is derived from the powerful language LISP used in artificial intelligence research.

8. T   F   The first educational software on the market was inadequate.

9. T   F   Some colleges require that all students buy a microcomputer, usually offered at a discounted price through the school.

10. T   F   Originally, computers were used on campus strictly for word-processing tasks.

MATCHING

DIRECTIONS: *Read each question carefully. Choose the correct answer from the list below and write the letter of the answer in the space provided.*

a. BASIC
b. Pascal
c. Logo
d. objectives
e. videodisc
f. software

g. hardware
h. computer-assisted instruction
i. incentives
j. computer training

1. One problem with trying to define computer literacy in terms of specific _____ is that they are constantly changing as the technology changes.

2. Teachers need _____ for training in computers because they often are skeptical of the computer's new role in education.

3. For educators, _____ is never over because of the changing nature of the technology.

4. The use of a computer to instruct a student is known as _____ .

5. New _____ technology is making possible educational programs with movie-like sound and motion.

6. Bad programming techniques may be encouraged by _____ .

7. A derivative of LISP often used to instruct young children is _____ .

8. When educators first were bringing computers into the classroom, they tended not to allocate enough funds for _____ .

9. Manufacturers are offering _____ discounts to many students who are required to buy their own computers.

10. A popular programming language for high school students that is widely accepted and encourages the use of structured programming is _____ .

SHORT ANSWER

DIRECTIONS: *Read each question carefully. Answer each question using three or four complete sentences.*

1. How are technological changes affecting computer literacy programs in education?

2. Why do teachers need incentives for computer training?

3.   What makes the computer a good "teacher?"

4.   What advantage does CAI have over traditional discussion methods in classes with large numbers of students?

5.   When a school is equipped with a communication system using micrcomputers in conjunction with telecommunication equipment and services, in what types of educational activities can students engage?

6.   What programming language is particularly effective in teaching young children programming skills? Why is it effective with children?

7. What mistake did educators frequently make in planning for the implementation of early school computer systems?

8. What is one factor on which the success of the South Brunswick, New Jersey, school system could be based?

9. How are Apple, IBM, Digital Equipment Corporation (DEC), and Zenith aiding the computer education programs in universities across the country?

10. Explain the advantages and disadvantages of both BASIC and Pascal as programming languages for high school students.

ANSWER KEY
True/False
1. F   **3.** T   **5.** F   **7.** F   **9.** T

Matching
1. d   **3.** j   **5.** e   **7.** c   **9.** g

Short Answer Suggested Responses
Your answers for the odd questions should contain most of the information below.

1. The objectives of computer literacy programs are constantly changing to keep pace with advancing technology. This makes computer literacy programs difficult to implement in education systems.

3. CAI programs are patient teachers, presenting materials at a pace set by the students and providing them with immediate feedback for their answers.

5. Students can access information services to send and receive electronic mail, or they can consult on-line encyclopedias, reducing research time. Students also can link with other schools, allowing them to exchange games, newsletters, and student-written programs.

7. Early in the computer literacy drive, educational administrators frequently invested millions of dollars in hardware and training while software to support the new equipment often was inadequate. In their rush to get the latest technology for the least money, educators often found themselves without a well-thought-out plan for using their purchases. Moreover, schools often lacked personnel with sufficient knowledge to select appropriate software.

9. These companies are offering schools substantial discounts on hardware. At some schools where ownership of a microcomputer is mandatory, students are offered considerable discounts as well.

Chapter 12
Computers in Science, Medicine, And Research and Design

SUMMARY

Scientists use computers to perform calculations, simulate real situations, and observe equipment and conditions involved in research.

Scientists use computers to monitor the environment by providing storage and manipulation of enormous amounts of data. The monitoring of NASA-launched Landsat satellite pictures is a constant activity. The pictures can be analyzed by computers to help scientists locate areas of unhealthy vegetation, mineral or oil deposits, or places with insect infestation or drought problems.

Computers are used to monitor air-traffic and space-flight operations. Emergency management systems might prevent, in the future, accidents such as those at the Union Carbide chemical plant in Bhopal, India, and the accident at the Three Mile Island nuclear power plant. In the event of an emergency, these systems are capable of monitoring the danger to the surrounding population and environment. The computers involved can even phone residents in affected areas, warning them and facilitating evacuation if necessary.

Artificial-intelligence software can help geologists locate likely oil deposits, eliminating time and money spent drilling dry wells. Weather forecasting utilizes a complex system of 14 computers in communication with hundreds of data collection programs around the world, as well as four satellites.

Many scientific instruments are controlled by computer. Experiments that involve the synthesizing of DNA have been made faster, easier, and less expensive with computer control. Volcanoes are monitored by computer-controlled devices. Unmanned undersea exploration probes also are being controlled successfully by computer.

In the field of medicine, computers are being used to perform a multitude of tasks. Record-keeping tasks are handled much more efficiently by computer methods than by traditional manual means. Computers also keep track of blood banks, plan patient meals, and compile medical histories of patients. Through multiphasic health testing, computerized axial tomography, and magnetic resonance imaging, computers are helping doctors to diagnose conditions that used to require surgery. Even treatments are aided by computers. Pacemakers, microprocessors controlling artificial limbs, programmable implantable medicine systems, and computer-controlled lasers all are computerized methods utilizing computers that physicians use in treating patients.

Computers are proving invaluable to researchers in all fields, including language and legal research. Scientists are using computers to help them learn to communicate with dolphins. Artificial joints are being designed with the aid of computers. Computers are even allowing anthropologists to recreate the faces of mummies thousands of years old, and doctors to recreate the faces and skulls of patients requiring reconstructive surgery.

STRUCTURED LEARNING

DIRECTIONS: *First, use a blank sheet of paper to cover the answer, without reading it. Then read the question carefully and write the letter of the correct answer in the space provided. Uncover the answer to see if you chose the correct response.*

1. Landsat satellite pictures are recorded as _____ .
a. analog pulses
b. digital pulses
c. radiation
d. laser images

◊ ◊ ◊ ◊ ◊ ◊ ◊ ◊ ◊ ◊ ◊ ◊ ◊ ◊ ◊ ◊ ◊ ◊ ◊ ◊

    b.   digital pulses. The digitized electronic pulses are broadcast to receiving stations on the ground and then translated into photographs by a computer.

2. A Landsat photo with a predominately red hue would indicate _____ .
a. healthy vegetation
b. insect infestation
c. drought
d. urban areas

◊ ◊ ◊ ◊ ◊ ◊ ◊ ◊ ◊ ◊ ◊ ◊ ◊ ◊ ◊ ◊ ◊ ◊ ◊ ◊

    a.   healthy vegetation. Healthy plants emit a high level of infrared radiation, which appears as a red hue on a Landsat photo. Urban areas emit much less radiation, so they appear as a grayish-blue color.

3. A(n) _____ utilizes computers to monitor chemical plants or nuclear power plants to help prevent accidents such as the one at the Union Carbide plant in Bhopal, India.

a. evacuation management system

b. chemical management system

c. fallout management system

d. emergency management system

◊ ◊ ◊ ◊ ◊ ◊ ◊ ◊ ◊ ◊ ◊ ◊ ◊ ◊ ◊ ◊ ◊ ◊ ◊

d. emergency management system. Emergency management systems monitor temperature, toxin levels, and wind direction and velocity around a plant using sensors connected to a central computer. In an emergency, contigency plans have already mapped out by the computer are activated. The computer can even telephone nearby residents, warning them of danger and facilitating evacuation if necessary.

4. The Dipmeter Advisor is an example of a(n) _____ .

a. data-collection program (DCP)

b. emergency management system

c. expert system

d. seismometer

◊ ◊ ◊ ◊ ◊ ◊ ◊ ◊ ◊ ◊ ◊ ◊ ◊ ◊ ◊ ◊ ◊ ◊ ◊

c. expert system. The Dipmeter Advisor is designed to imitate an expert in the choice of sites to drill for oil.

5. Computers first were introduced in the field of medicine to _____ .

a. perform diagnosis

b. handle record keeping

c. plan patient meals

d. compile medical histories of patients

◊ ◊ ◊ ◊ ◊ ◊ ◊ ◊ ◊ ◊ ◊ ◊ ◊ ◊ ◊ ◊ ◊ ◊ ◊

b. handle record keeping. Record-keeping procedures at a large hospital strongly resemble those of a corporation. Computers first were used to simplify this task.

6. _____ joins X-rays and computerized evaluations of X-rays.
a.   Multiphasic health testing
b.   Computerized axial tomography
c.   Computer-aided monitoring
d.   Magnetic resonance imaging

◊ ◊ ◊ ◊ ◊ ◊ ◊ ◊ ◊ ◊ ◊ ◊ ◊ ◊ ◊ ◊ ◊ ◊ ◊

b.   Computerized axial tomography. CAT scans provide clear pictures of cross-sections of the body. They often are used to aid doctors in reconstructive surgery.

7. _____ techniques can resolve images of soft-tissue areas such as muscles and nerves.
a.   Computerized axial tomography
b.   Multiphasic health testing
c.   Magnetic resonance imaging
d.   Electromagnetic pulse scanning

◊ ◊ ◊ ◊ ◊ ◊ ◊ ◊ ◊ ◊ ◊ ◊ ◊ ◊ ◊ ◊ ◊ ◊ ◊

c.   Magnetic resonance imaging. MRI techniques can provide a physician with information on the state of soft- or nerve-tissue areas within a human body.

8. A small computer that releases drugs internally over a period of time is called a _____ .
a.   programmable implantable medicine system
b.   pacemaker
c.   radio telemetry medicine system
d.   computer-aided implantable medicine system

◊ ◊ ◊ ◊ ◊ ◊ ◊ ◊ ◊ ◊ ◊ ◊ ◊ ◊ ◊ ◊ ◊ ◊ ◊

a.   programmable implantable medicine systems. A PIMS device provides constant, even doses of medication such as insulin for patients who require daily administering.

9. In many cases, round-the-clock nursing for individual patients in intensive care is no longer necessary due to _____ .
a.   multiphasic health testing
b.   computerized axial tomography
c.   computer-assisted treatment
d.   computer-aided monitoring

◊ ◊ ◊ ◊ ◊ ◊ ◊ ◊ ◊ ◊ ◊ ◊ ◊ ◊ ◊ ◊ ◊ ◊

d. computer-aided monitoring. Computer-controlled machines monitor life-support systems. They inform doctors and nurses of vital signs such as heartbeat, blood pressure, respiration, and temperature. Alarms are sounded if dangerous conditions arise.

10. A database containing rabbinical statements and judgments on legal questions is called the _____ .
a. Hebrew Judgment Log
b. Hebrew Scholar Project
c. Responsa Project
d. Legal Response Bank

◊ ◊ ◊ ◊ ◊ ◊ ◊ ◊ ◊ ◊ ◊ ◊ ◊ ◊ ◊ ◊ ◊ ◊

c. Responsa Project. The Responsa Project is a database of questions and answers about religious issues. It provides a base for the Israeli legal system and provides historians with an invaluable guide to Jewish life since the Middle Ages.

TRUE/FALSE

DIRECTIONS: *Read each question carefully, then circle either T or F to correctly answer each question.*

1. T F Landsat is the name for the NASA supported, National Weather Service satellite system.

2. T F Landsat photos can be used to locate the best sites for oil drilling.

3. T F The castrophe following the gas leak at the Union Carbide plant in Bhopal, India, was in large part the fault of a malfunctioning emergency management system.

4. T F The Dipmeter Advisor is actually a form of artificial-intelligence software.

5. T F Because of the critical decisions that must be made, computers are virtually useless in the synthesizing of DNA.

6. T F The wreck of the Titanic was discovered by a submerged IBM PC/AT microcomputer.

7. T F A computer-aided diagnosis database was the first computer application found for computers in the medical field.

8.   T   F   The May, 1980, eruption of the Mount St. Helens volcano in Washington was predicted by scientists with the help of data analyzed by computers.

9.   T   F   Magnetic resonance imaging examinations produce more definitive and valuable information than CAT scans in determining the presence of inner-ear or brain tumors.

10.   T   F   Computer-powered PIMS devices have replaced primitive, unwieldy pacemakers.

MATCHING

DIRECTIONS: *Read each question carefully. Choose the correct answer from the list below and write the letter of the answer in the space provided.*

a.   programmable implantable medicine systems
b.   multiphasic health testing
c.   emergency management systems
d.   computerized axial tomography
e.   magnetic resonance imaging
f.   data-collection programs
g.   seismometers
h.   computer-assisted treatment
i.   infrared radiation
j.   computer-controlled lasers

1.   Areas of healthy and sick vegetation can be identified by examining the _____ patterns on Landsat pictures.

2.   The Federal Nuclear Regulatory Commission requires _____ in nuclear power plants.

3.   The National Weather Service collects information from weather stations, satellites, and worldwide _____ .

4.   Volcanic eruptions can be accurately predicted with the help of data collected by _____, which measure tremors in the vicinity of the volcano.

5.   Procedures in _____ include electrocardiograms, X-rays, blood tests, vision and hearing tests, blood-pressure tests, and height and weight measurements.

6.   X-rays and computerized evaluations of X-rays are joined in _____ .

7.   An important advantage to _____ examinations is that they do not expose patients to radiation.

8. Some of the life-threatening side effects of diabetes may be eliminated through the use of _____ .

9. A nonsurgical treatment for kidney stones involves the use of _____ .

10. Improved pacemakers designed to accommodate individual patients' particular heart problems are an example of _____ techniques.

SHORT ANSWER

DIRECTIONS: *Read each question carefully. Answer each question using three or four complete sentences.*

1. How are the pictures from Landsat satellites recorded and transmitted to earth?

2. What two situations mentioned in the text might have been prevented by emergency management systems?

3.   What constitutes the National Weather Service's "brain"?

4.   How can computers predict volcanic eruptions?

5.   How are computers used to obtain the medical histories of patients?

6.   Computers increasingly are being combined with medical testing equipment to provide diagnostic tools. Name three forms of these tools.

7. In what way are magnetic resonance imaging techniques an improvement over standard X-rays (radiography)?

8. How do computers assist in the design and manufacture of artificial joints for humans?

9. In addition to scholars, what other groups make use of the information contained in the Responsa Project database?

10. How are computers being used to communicate with dolphins?

ANSWER KEY

True/False

1. F   3. F   5. F   7. F   9. T

Matching

1. i   3. f   5. b   7. e   9. j

Short Answer Suggested Responses

Your answers for the odd questions should contain most of the information below.

1. The pictures are recorded as digitized electronic pulses which are broadcast to earth receiving stations. When received, they are translated into photographs by a computer.

3. The "brain" consists of 14 computers housed at the meteorological center in Maryland, which collects data from DCPs, weather stations, and weather satellites.

5. Patients are "interviewed" by a computer. Patients are presented with questions and they respond by focusing a light pen on the correct answer on the monitor screen. Often patients are more comfortable dealing with computers in this capacity than with doctors or nurses.

7. MRI procedures can resolve images of soft tissue areas that do not show up in radiography.

9. Sociologists, historians, economists, linguists, and lawyers all make use of the information contained in the rabbinical statements and judgments on legal questions.

Chapter 13

Computers in Art, Entertainment, and Sports

SUMMARY

Computers are making an impact on society outside of the offices and factories where they have revolutionized the world of work. Their presence in the arts and in leisure activities is growing.

Computers have made their debut on Broadway—handling complex lighting for such Tony Award winning shows as *A Chorus Line* and *Dream Girls*. Lincoln Center, home of New York City's Metropolitan Opera, has a computer-controlled lighting system as well.

In ballet, computers are being used for dance notation, the mapping of complex dance movements. Computer graphics also allow dancers and choreographers to translate dancers' motions into moving figures on a computer screen that can then be studied and analyzed.

Writers have harnessed the computer as much or more than other artists. The word processor has made the task of writing, editing, and rewriting much easier than with the traditional typewriter. Writers now use computers at virtually all newspapers and magazines. Thousands of full-length books have been written on computers. Computer professionals have even devised programs that generate poetic verses. The outputs are regarded as humorous. However, scholars are able to study the style and technique of famous writers in great detail through the use of computers.

Modern music owes a great deal to the computer. A synthesizer can reproduce the sound of practically any instrument, besides being able to produce sounds unique to itself. Computers can effectively edit recordings as well. The ability of computers to generate musical scores can save time and money. Many television commercials contain computer-generated music.

The computer screen provides a flexible canvas for visual artists. Computer graphics are being applied to generate outputs which are considered an emerging art form. Using electronic pens or joysticks, computer artists can draw pictures, retouch photos, and create television graphics. Three-dimensional models can be produced on the monitor screen to serve as models for paintings and sculptures. Saul Bernstein is one of the leading computer artists.

In filmmaking, computers are used in a number of applications. Scriptwriting, particularly for television, requires many rewrites, and the word processor makes rewriting a much simpler task than it is with a typewriter. Computers also can generate sound effects and visual special effects. Animation has particularly benefited from the introduction of computers. The computer can easily duplicate backgrounds and foregrounds for image frames and can move characters through them in a lifelike manner.

Even sports have changed as a result of computer technology. Statistics are compiled and analyzed by computers. These statistics are then supplied to coaches for strategy planning, to scouts for recruiting purposes, and to fans for the sake of argument. Computers are used to schedule sporting events. They are used to determine handicaps for golfers at private and public courses. Computers are used to rank tennis players and as line judges in major professional tennis matches. Competitive bicyclists use computer-designed, aerodynamic helmets and computer-controlled sensors to improve performance.

Biomechanics is a science that studies the movements of athletes. Using computer images of a performing athlete, coaches and trainers can help the athlete optimize performance.

STRUCTURED LEARNING

DIRECTIONS: *First, use a blank sheet of paper to cover the answer, without reading it. Then read the question carefully and write the letter of the correct answer in the space provided. Uncover the answer to see if you chose the correct response.*

1. The computer lighting system used in *A Chorus Line* and in the Lincoln Center for Metropolitan Opera productions is called _____ .
   a. Broadway Lighting System
   b. Light Palette
   c. Dream Palette
   d. Gaslight Systems

◊ ◊ ◊ ◊ ◊ ◊ ◊ ◊ ◊ ◊ ◊ ◊ ◊ ◊ ◊ ◊ ◊ ◊

   b. Light Palette. The software of this system makes available more than 30,000 lighting options from which one operator can choose with a keystroke.

2. Computers are used in ballet for _____ .
   a. costume design
   b. dance notation
   c. instruction
   d. videotape enhancement

◊ ◊ ◊ ◊ ◊ ◊ ◊ ◊ ◊ ◊ ◊ ◊ ◊ ◊ ◊ ◊ ◊ ◊ ◊

  b. dance notation. This application involves the "mapping" of dance movements, which are translated by computer graphics into figures moving on a monitor screen.

3. Computer-generated poetry can help scholars to study the _____ of famous writers.

a. behavioral patterns

b. inspirational sources

c. style and technique

d. religious beliefs

◊ ◊ ◊ ◊ ◊ ◊ ◊ ◊ ◊ ◊ ◊ ◊ ◊ ◊ ◊ ◊ ◊ ◊ ◊

  c. style and technique. Scholars are able to study the style and technique of famous writers in great detail through the use of computers.

4. The electronic synthesizer _____ to produce unique sounds.

a. simulates sound waves

b. eliminates sound waves

c. bends sound waves

d. amplifies sound waves

◊ ◊ ◊ ◊ ◊ ◊ ◊ ◊ ◊ ◊ ◊ ◊ ◊ ◊ ◊ ◊ ◊ ◊ ◊

  c. bends sound waves. The synthesizer also can imitate any musical instrument.

5. A computer artist must possess a thorough knowledge of the capabilities of _____ .

a. primary storage

b. animation

c. plotters and scanners

d. drawing and painting software

◊ ◊ ◊ ◊ ◊ ◊ ◊ ◊ ◊ ◊ ◊ ◊ ◊ ◊ ◊ ◊ ◊ ◊

d.   drawing and painting software. Knowing about drawing and painting software is, for the computer artist, the equivalent of knowing about different brush, pen, and paint types.

6.   Writers who use word processing for scriptwriting are able to _____ .
a.   make revisions with ease
b.   emulate other writers' styles
c.   eliminate editing
d.   write shorter scripts

◊ ◊ ◊ ◊ ◊ ◊ ◊ ◊ ◊ ◊ ◊ ◊ ◊ ◊ ◊ ◊ ◊ ◊

a.   make revisions with ease. Scripts are scrutinized closely and changed frequently. Revisions used to require retyping. Now, the scripts are revised and output from computers.

7.   Disney's system for approximating human motions in animation is called _____ .
a.   ACCESS
b.   ACES
c.   Audio-Animatronics
d.   Auto-Animation

◊ ◊ ◊ ◊ ◊ ◊ ◊ ◊ ◊ ◊ ◊ ◊ ◊ ◊ ◊ ◊ ◊ ◊

c.   Audio-Animatronics. The system provides cartoon characters with humanlike movement and also coordinates the movements with voices and music.

8.   The official compiler of statistics for the National Baseball League is _____ .
a.   the Elias Sports Bureau
b.   ABC
c.   United Scouting Combine (USC)
d.   Holly and Henry Stephenson

◊ ◊ ◊ ◊ ◊ ◊ ◊ ◊ ◊ ◊ ◊ ◊ ◊ ◊ ◊ ◊ ◊ ◊

a.   The Elias Sports Bureau. This firm uses an enormous database to compile and distribute statistics.

9. The electronic eye used to make line judgments in professional tennis tournaments is known as _____ .
a. Monocle
b. Electroserve
c. Compuserve
d. Cyclops

◊ ◊ ◊ ◊ ◊ ◊ ◊ ◊ ◊ ◊ ◊ ◊ ◊ ◊ ◊ ◊ ◊ ◊

d. Cyclops. The electronic eye, nicknamed Cyclops, is used as a service-line referee during tournaments.

10. The science dealing with the movements of athletes is _____ .
a. biofeedback
b. biomechanics
c. biodigital analysis
d. biodigitology

◊ ◊ ◊ ◊ ◊ ◊ ◊ ◊ ◊ ◊ ◊ ◊ ◊ ◊ ◊ ◊ ◊ ◊

b. biomechanics. By analyzing frame by frame stick-figure images of athletes in action, biomechanical engineers can help them improve their performance.

TRUE/FALSE

DIRECTIONS: *Read each question carefully, then circle either T or F to correctly answer each question.*

1. T   F   The Lincoln Center, home of the Metropolitan Opera, has a complex computer-controlled gas lighting system.

2. T   F   Computers are being used by linguistic scholars to study word, rhyme, and language patterns.

3. T   F   The electronic synthesizer generates sound by using recordings of musical instruments which are distorted through the circuitry of an internal microprocessor.

4. T   F   Saul Bernstein is one of the foremost electronic musicians today.

5. T   F   Knowledge of computer hardware and graphics tools is not necessary for the computer artist to generate artwork.

6.   T   F   ACCESS is a sound effects library that includes sounds that range from an automobile crash to chirping crickets.

7.   T   F   Using computer animation systems, artists have to draw only the front, side, and top view of objects to be animated; the computer completes the object so that it can be moved and rotated in space on the monitor screen.

8.   T   F   The United Scouting Combine uses computers to compile statistics on every player signed by any National Football League team.

9.   T   F   NFL teams whose coaches use computers on the sidelines win much more often than those who do not.

10.   T   F   Most rides and many of the shows presented in theme parks such as Disneyland, Disney World, and Universal Studios are supported by computers.

MATCHING

DIRECTIONS: *Read each question carefully. Choose the correct answer from the list below and write the letter of the answer in the space provided.*

a.   search and search/replace   f.   illiterate art
b.   sound effects   g.   digital synthesizer
c.   game strategy   h.   joystick
d.   calculating statistics   i.   word processing
e.   revision   j.   vocabulary

1.   Choreographers employ _____ in dance notation.

2.   Choreographers often speak of dance as the _____ .

3.   To write poetry, a computer requires a program and a(n) _____ .

4.   Thomas Dolby uses a(n) _____ called a Fairlight to assist in the creation of original musical compositions.

5.   The computer artist paints with a(n) _____ .

6.   Because scripts for television sitcoms need _____ constantly, the computer is becoming a major tool in Hollywood.

7. Writers can locate and make changes to particular passages or words within a manuscript by using the _____ capabilities of a computer.

8. In addition to capabilities for reproduction of specific instruments, computers also produce other _____ , such as stones scraping the pavement or glass breaking.

9. In sports, computers are used for _____ .

10. A controversial use of computers in football involves using the equipment to access information useful for determining _____ .

SHORT ANSWER

DIRECTIONS: *Read each question carefully. Answer each question using three or four complete sentences.*

1. What is Light Palette?

2. Ballet is often called the illiterate art by choreographers. Explain how it got the title and how the computer is helping it to become literate.

3. How do linguistic scholars use computers?

4.   How do computers facilitate the writing and publishing of news-
paper articles?

5.   How does the electronic synthesizer create unique sounds?

6.   Who is Saul Bernstein?

7.   How are computers used in making movies?

8. What are some uses of computers in professional sports?

9. Why is computer use by the coaching staff banned during professional football games?

10. How are computers helping individual athletes improve their performances?

ANSWER KEY

True/False

1. F   3. F   5. F   7. T   9. F

Matching

1. i   3. j   5. h   7. a   9. d

Short Answer Suggested Responses

Your answers for the odd questions should contain most of the information below.

1. Light Palette is a lighting system that controls complex lighting effects with a computer.

3. Computers are being used by linguistic scholars to study word, rhyme, and language patterns. A computer can provide detailed information regarding such factors as syllable patterns and word usage within literary works.

5. The electronic synthesizer creates new sounds by bending sound waves.

7. Word processing often is used to produce scripts and subsequent rewrites. Computer systems generate special effects. ACCESS is a disk library and editing system used in sound editing. Computers may be used to generate animation and for film and video editing.

9. The use of computers by coaches during games has been forbidden in the NFL because it is felt that coaches with access to computers would have an unfair advantage over those who do not.

Chapter 14
Computers and the Law:
Government, Privacy, Security,
And Copyright

SUMMARY

The government is the largest user of computer systems in the United States. Government applications include information storage and retrieval, military planning, and fire prevention.

The U.S. census, taken every 10 years, is an example of an information-collecting task that could not be performed without computers. Computers are used to maintain files containing the names and addresses of the majority of United States citizens. Answers collected on census forms are then collected in large databases. The government is responsible for safeguarding the collected information against misuse.

In the military, computers are used to keep records of personnel, to plan defenses, to practice battle strategies, and to maintain watch over offensive maneuvers. NORAD uses an enormous database to help it analyze possible missile attacks from anywhere in the world. Computers can also simulate war, helping officers to experience simulated combat situations.

The National Bureau of Standards uses computers to build models of potential fire sites and to help devise evacuation paths for people who might be in the buildings modeled. The U.S. Bureau of Land Management uses a lightning-alert system to help prevent forest fires.

The government is also responsible for three of the largest databases. The Library of Congress has its huge catalog of books in a database. The Federal Bureau of Investigation has a comprehensive network of information about criminals and suspects. The Internal Revenue Service has financial records on anyone who earns enough money to be taxed. Other government systems include the nation's air-traffic-control system and the database used by the Social Security Administration.

Computers have become major tools for support of legislative processes at the federal and state levels. They are used to record new laws and to determine instances wherein new laws supersede existing laws.

Invasion of privacy has become a major issue surrounding the use of databases. The efficiency of computers has made it easy for government and business offices to gather too much information about citizens or customers and to share that information. It is also difficult to keep information in databases secure from outsiders who might use the information in ways that could be harmful to the people the information is about.

A number of recent laws regulate access to information in databases. On the federal level, the Freedom of Information Act of 1970, the Fair Credit Reporting Act of 1970, the Privacy Act of 1978, and the Comprehensive Crime Control Act of 1984 are all laws designed to protect, in some way, the privacy of individuals whose personal information is stored in databases.

Many states have enacted legislation, based on the federal Privacy Act of 1974, to protect innocent citizens from harm due the misuse of information from databases. Differences in laws from state to state revolve around the differing definitions applied to legal terms.

Computers are being used both to prevent and commit crimes. Statistical analysis has provided law enforcement agencies with information about sites for potential arson. The FBI has a computerized crime predictor that is efficient in tracking down criminals. These systems, in conjunction with others, are helping to track down mass murdurers and terrorists. Many people, however, are worried that the system will be used to keep track of innocent citizens, in effect, exercising control over them.

Computers are used by the courts to keep track of scheduling, for word processing, for special programs to keep track of juvenile offenders, and for research. A research service called WESTLAW has been designed to aid lawyers and judges in legal research. Inslaw, a computer software company, has created program packages to streamline the administrative task of keeping track of people who pass through the judicial system.

Computer crime is defined, in practical terms, as a criminal act that poses a greater threat to computer owners than to nonowners or a crime that is accomplished through use of a computer. There are four basic kinds of computer crime: sabotage, theft of services, property crimes, and financial crimes. Sabotage involves the destruction of property. Computer services can be abused by employees acquiring lists of names from databases for their own use, or by outside users wire-tapping to gain free services. In property crimes, hardware itself is stolen, or software is stolen or illegally copied. Financial crimes committed with computers are many and varied. Employees often use their access to company or government financial information to embezzle funds.

Illegal duplication of software is a widespread problem. The law, in general, holds that it is illegal to duplicate and use disks that contain software covered by copyright. If the developer does grant copy permission, it usually applies only to one duplicate, working disk.

STRUCTURED LEARNING

DIRECTIONS: *First, use a blank sheet of paper to cover the answer, without reading it. Then read the question carefully and write the letter of the correct answer in the space provided. Uncover the answer to see if you chose the correct response.*

1. Within seconds after they are launched, the positions of rockets and missiles anywhere in the world can be calculated by computers at _____ .

a. Janus
b. NORAD
c. NAVTAG
d. NRC

◊ ◊ ◊ ◊ ◊ ◊ ◊ ◊ ◊ ◊ ◊ ◊ ◊ ◊ ◊ ◊ ◊ ◊

    b.   NORAD. The North America Air Defense Command near Colorado Springs has an enormous database for military control purposes.

2. A nuclear war can be simulated by a program called _____ .
a. Janus
b. Star Wars
c. NAVTAG
d. NORAD

◊ ◊ ◊ ◊ ◊ ◊ ◊ ◊ ◊ ◊ ◊ ◊ ◊ ◊ ◊ ◊ ◊ ◊

    a.   Janus. The program is used to train high-ranking officers for command positions.

3. The U.S. Navy has developed a game called _____ that serves as a training device to enhance preparedness in military actions.
a. Star Wars
b. NAVSTRAT
c. NAVTAG
d. Naval Strategy

◊ ◊ ◊ ◊ ◊ ◊ ◊ ◊ ◊ ◊ ◊ ◊ ◊ ◊ ◊ ◊ ◊ ◊

    c.   NAVTAG. Officers gain valuable experience in decision making under stress.

4. When government records were kept manually, privacy was best protected by _____ .

a.   federal legislation
b.   state legislation
c.   personal ethics
d.   inefficiency

◊ ◊ ◊ ◊ ◊ ◊ ◊ ◊ ◊ ◊ ◊ ◊ ◊ ◊ ◊ ◊ ◊ ◊

    d.   inefficiency. When government records were kept manually, files tended to be widely dispersed, and each file tended to have information relevant only to the keeper of that particular file. Access to information in these files was generally very limited as well.

5. The _____ allows individuals to access data about themselves in files collected by federal agencies.

a.   Fair Credit Reporting Act of 1970
b.   Freedom of Information Act of 1970
c.   Privacy Act of 1974
d.   Right to Financial Privacy Act of 1978

◊ ◊ ◊ ◊ ◊ ◊ ◊ ◊ ◊ ◊ ◊ ◊ ◊ ◊ ◊ ◊ ◊ ◊

    b.   The Freedom of Information Act of 1970. This was one of the first federal laws to address the problem of information abuse.

6. The FBI's National Crime Information Center can be used by _____ to keep track of people who are considered threats to public figures.

a.   civil libertarians
b.   private citizens
c.   the Secret Service
d.   journalists

◊ ◊ ◊ ◊ ◊ ◊ ◊ ◊ ◊ ◊ ◊ ◊ ◊ ◊ ◊ ◊ ◊ ◊

    c.   the Secret Service. This agency is in charge of protecting the president and other government officials and foreign dignitaries. The FBI's computer systems help agents to watch people who might be dangerous to those the FBI must protect.

7. A research service, based in St. Paul, designed for use by judges and lawyers is called _____ .
a. WESTLAW
b. Inslaw
c. LAWFILE
d. CASEFILE

◊ ◊ ◊ ◊ ◊ ◊ ◊ ◊ ◊ ◊ ◊ ◊ ◊ ◊ ◊ ◊ ◊ ◊

    a. WESTLAW. West Publishing created WESTLAW to aid judges and lawyers in finding legal precedents that might have bearing on current cases.

8. A profile of the typical computer criminal has been compiled which indicates that computer crime within large companies is often perpetrated by _____ .
a. workers with criminal backgrounds
b. employees turned down for promotions
c. ambitious, well-educated, "model" employees
d. workers with limited computer experience

◊ ◊ ◊ ◊ ◊ ◊ ◊ ◊ ◊ ◊ ◊ ◊ ◊ ◊ ◊ ◊ ◊ ◊

    c. ambitious, well-educated, "model" employees. Often, the criminal appears to be a perfect employee—young, ambitious, and possessing impressive educational credentials. He or she may be a technician, programmer, manager, or high-ranking executive.

9. Which of the following is *not* one of the four basic categories of computer crime? _____
a. sabotage
b. theft of services
c. ethical crimes
d. financial crimes

◊ ◊ ◊ ◊ ◊ ◊ ◊ ◊ ◊ ◊ ◊ ◊ ◊ ◊ ◊ ◊ ◊ ◊

    c. ethical crimes. The other category of computer crime is property crimes—the theft of hardware, or the theft or illegal copying of software.

10. The standard of moral conduct in computer use is referred to as _____ .

a.   computer security
b.   computer ethics
c.   computer privacy
d.   computer legislation

◊ ◊ ◊ ◊ ◊ ◊ ◊ ◊ ◊ ◊ ◊ ◊ ◊ ◊ ◊ ◊ ◊ ◊ ◊

b.   computer ethics. The security of computer data ultimately depends on ethical behavior.

TRUE/FALSE

DIRECTIONS: *Read each question carefully, then circle either T or F to correctly answer each question.*

1.   T   F   The biggest user of computers in the United States is the federal government.

2.   T   F   NORAD is a computer program used to simulate nuclear war in training high-ranking officers for command positions.

3.   T   F   In California, the U.S. Bureau of Land Management uses a system that detects and pinpoints the position of lightning strikes.

4.   T   F   By the year 2000, air traffic control in the U.S. will be advanced enough to fly commercial airplanes automatically, eliminating the need for human pilots.

5.   T   F   Before databases took over for many manual government filing systems, it was easier to compile a detailed dossier on an individual.

6.   T   F   Data kept in databases is much easier to keep secure than information stored in manual file systems.

7.   T   F   The only significant federal attempt to regulate the information practices of private organizations is the Fair Credit Reporting Act of 1970.

8.   T   F   The differences in state privacy laws are basically differences in how the violations or terms are defined.

9.   T   F   Computer crime involves acts that pose a greater threat to computers than to computer owners.

10.   T   F   Before computers took over information processing, most business and government decisions were based on personal knowledge and intuition.

MATCHING

DIRECTIONS: *Read each question carefully. Choose the correct answer from the list below and write the letter of the answer in the space provided.*

a. National Crime Information Center   f. computer crime
b. Privacy Act of 1974   g. legal precedents
c. identity   h. white-collar
d. NORAD   i. NAVTAG
e. Freedom of Information Act of 1970   j. antiterrorist

1. The _____ database accepts data from radar and satellite equipment all over the world.

2. A military training game that teaches players tactics and supplies them with real facts on the equipment and weapons of both sides is called _____ .

3. The _____ , a database maintained by the FBI, is linked to 64,000 federal, state, and local law enforcement agencies.

4. The French government has implemented a(n) _____ database containing information from a number of legal agencies concerned with border security, military security, and terrorism.

5. The most sweeping federal legislation designed to protect the privacy of citizens is the _____ .

6. The _____ was passed because of the potential for the government to conceal its proceedings from the public.

7. In the judicial system, computers are used to gather and compare evidence for trial, and to aid in jury selection, record keeping, and searches for _____ .

8. Because computer crimes often are committed by professional people or office employees, they are called _____ crimes.

9. The unique threat of computer crime is that criminals often use computers to conceal their _____ and the existence of the crimes.

10. Making unauthorized copies of computer software is considered a(n) _____ .

SHORT ANSWER

DIRECTIONS: *Read each question carefully. Answer each question using three or four complete sentences.*

1. What are some ways that the U.S. military uses computers?

2. What is Janus and why is it important in training officers for command positions?

3. Outline the ways in which the FBI is making use of computers.

4. What is the significance of the Freedom of Information Act of 1970?

5. What is the significance of the Fair Credit Reporting Act of 1970?

6. How is privacy litigation a "contradiction in terms"?

7. What factors can help explain the prevalence of computer crime?

8. Why are computer crimes often referred to as white-collar crimes?

9. How can software developers protect their copyrighted programs?

10. Ultimately, what is the only true safeguard against the misuse of computer data?

ANSWER KEY

True/False

1. T   3. T   5. F   7. T   9. F

Matching

1. d   3. a   5. b   7. g   9. c

Short Answer Suggested Responses

Your answers for the odd questions should contain most of the information below.

1. Some of the military uses for computers are to keep records, to monitor rocket or missile launchings anywhere in the world, to simulate nuclear war, and to train soldiers through the use of electronic war games.

3. The FBI has one of the largest databases in the U.S. The agency has a number of different computer systems to aid them in crime detection and prevention. The FBI's National Crime Information Center connects 64,000 federal, state, and local law enforcement offices.

5. Passage of the Fair Credit Reporting Act of 1970 has been the only significant effort on the part of the federal government to regulate the information management practices of private organizations.

7. Reasons which may help explain the prevalence of computer crime include: lax security in data-processing areas; the intrinsic flexibility of computers; the spread of microcomputers and their simplified operating instructions; computer skills being taught to students at any early age; and the ease with which a lot of sensitive data can be accessed.

9. To protect their copyrighted programs, some developers release their software on "copy-protected" disks. These disks contain special coding in the directory tracks that make it impossible to copy them through standard modules that come with an operating system. However, these protective measures have been countered by other software houses which, while they do not endorse illegal copying, nonetheless have developed special software programs that make it possible to unlock and copy protected disks.

Chapter 15
Computers and the Future

SUMMARY

The rapid increase in computer power over the last 20 years has been due, in large part, to the increase in the number of circuits that can be packed onto a single microchip. Scientists anticipate the development of memory chips with capacities of 4 and 8 megabits in the near future.

Packing many circuits on a single chip speeds up computing by reducing the distance that electrical current must travel. This, however, causes four problems: heat generation, the crowding of input/output pins, crosstalk, and the danger that dust particles might block conducting paths.

Newer approaches to the heat dissipation problem use superconductivity and light-based processing. These approaches also promise to contribute to increases in processing speeds.

Superconductivity is based on the principle that, as conductors are brought to temperatures approaching absolute zero, resistance to electrical current disappears. Experiments are being conducted that are aimed at producing materials that will be superconductive at temperatures that approach normal room conditions. As superconductive materials become available, reductions in friction caused by the flow of electrons through carriers will reduce or eliminate the heat dissipation problem. Capabilities for processing data through transmission and recording of light-beam impulses also are anticipated. Light-based processing already is a major factor in the telecommunications field.

Gallium arsenide may replace silicon as the principal material for building chips. Chips made of gallium arsenide require lower voltages to operate, they conduct current five to seven times as fast as silicon chips, generate less heat, and produce less crosstalk. These chips are resistant to radiation as well.

The biochip is a theoretical chip grown from the proteins and enzymes of living material such as *E. coli* bacteria. Biochips would be 10 million times as powerful as today's microchips. And since they would be constructed of living material, they could repair and regenerate themselves.

Scientists and engineers also are working on new designs that could support development of faster and higher-capacity computers. These developments include associative memories, neural processors, and parallel processors.

An associative memory has built-in search capabilities that enable a computer to identify data items on the basis of content. Because associative memories are extremely fast, targeted data items can be located, potentially, in a few millionths of a second. Neural processors, under development, establish data and logic links by selecting paths in response to the types of problems being processed. In response to demands for increasingly higher capacities, designers are working on computers that incorporate multiple processors. This approach is known as parallel processing.

Up to now, the most powerful computers have been used for number crunching. However, artificial intelligence research is paving the way for more conceptual applications. More and more, computers and languages will begin to imitate human thought. Current AI programs are called expert systems, since they imitate procedures followed by a human expert in a given field, drawing conclusions and making recommendations based on a huge database. The use of nonmonotonic logic (which allows exceptions to assumptions) in building computer knowledge may be the key to bridging the gap between expert systems and true artificial intelligence. Script theory, which says that people generally have an idea of how to think in a given situation because of past experience, may also provide a foundation for such discovery.

Principles of AI can improve voice-recognition systems. Voice-recognition technology is still primitive. Systems in use today generally respond to a single voice. However, the study of spectrograms (computer-enhanced versions of the electrical waveforms of speech) has led to the isolation of sounds within words that everyone pronounces in the same manner. Speaker-independent systems could be developed with this technology. Data entry would be simplified through voice-recognition devices.

Robotics also will change as AI develops. Robots are still too primitive and too expensive to be practical for use around the home, but robots are available at a reasonable cost that are educational and fun to play with, such as the Topo robot. Turtle robots and the more complex RB5X are other robots on the family/educational market. Scientists are working hard to develop robots that are more mobile and sophisticated than those currently available.

In the future, all personal information—financial, medical, etc.— might be stored on a single card with a microchip embedded in its surface. Each person's card would control all of his or her funds. Purchases would involve immediate electronic funds transfers from the customer's account to the merchant's. The cards also could be used by the government to keep track of people and control what they do, since very little could be done without the card (which would serve as identification as well).

There are many concerns over what the use of databases may do to the printed word. Some people fear that children may not have the motivation to learn to read and write when computers respond to their speech and talk to them. Authors worry that their copyrighted works will be stolen from databases. The quality of information in databases is also under question. Information stored in a database is likely to be shaded by the biases of the person or organization that provided the information.

In the near future, it is likely that almost every job will require some knowledge of computers. Many people are not going to be prepared for this change, and these people will be disadvantaged in a computer-controlled Information Society. These people probably will be women, older people, or members of groups that are disadvantaged now. The public education system in this country is attempting to prepare children to meet the challenges of the society of the future.

STRUCTURED LEARNING

DIRECTIONS: *First, use a blank sheet of paper to cover the answer, without reading it. Then read the question carefully and write the letter of the correct answer in the space provided. Uncover the answer to see if you chose the correct response.*

1. Of the following, which is *not* a problem associated with packing more and more circuits on silicon chips? _____
a. heat generation
b. crowded input/output
c. crosstalk
d. reduced processing speeds

◊ ◊ ◊ ◊ ◊ ◊ ◊ ◊ ◊ ◊ ◊ ◊ ◊ ◊ ◊ ◊ ◊ ◊

    d. reduced processing speeds. Packing chips closer together improves the speed of processing by lessening the distance that the current must travel.

2. Chips made of _____ are five to seven times faster than silicon chips.
a. gallium arsenide
b. E. coli bacteria
c. liquid coolant
d. interferon

◊ ◊ ◊ ◊ ◊ ◊ ◊ ◊ ◊ ◊ ◊ ◊ ◊ ◊ ◊ ◊ ◊ ◊

    a. gallium arsenide. Chips made from this material also require less voltage to operate, generate less heat, create less crosstalk, and are resistant to radiation.

3. If developed, biochips will be grown from the proteins and enzymes of living material such as _____ .

a. nerve tissue
b. blood cells
c. E.coli bacteria
d. insulin

◊ ◊ ◊ ◊ ◊ ◊ ◊ ◊ ◊ ◊ ◊ ◊ ◊ ◊ ◊ ◊ ◊ ◊

c. E.coli bacteria. Like other life forms, they would require oxygen, and their signals would be most like those sent and transmitted through human nerve tissue.

4. To help minimize delays for software access, many computers use read-only hardware devices to store some system-software routines. These permanent programs have become known as _____ .

a. hardware
b. multiple processors
c. hard disks
d. firmware

◊ ◊ ◊ ◊ ◊ ◊ ◊ ◊ ◊ ◊ ◊ ◊ ◊ ◊ ◊ ◊ ◊ ◊

d. firmware. Instruction sets stored within hardware devices usually are used for startup procedures or other fast-response requirements.

5. Building computer knowledge may depend on the use of _____ , according to John McCarthy, an artificial intelligence researcher.

a. monotonic logic
b. nonmonotonic logic
c. voice recognition
d. neural processors

◊ ◊ ◊ ◊ ◊ ◊ ◊ ◊ ◊ ◊ ◊ ◊ ◊ ◊ ◊ ◊ ◊ ◊

b. nonmonotonic logic. This approach allows conclusions to be drawn from assumptions, even when added assumptions might make conclusions wrong. This may enable computers to allow for unusual situations.

6.   An approach to artificial intelligence that assumes humans have an advance idea of how to deal with a given situation is called _____ .

a.   monotonic logic

b.   natural logic

c.   script theory

d.   behavioral theory

◊ ◊ ◊ ◊ ◊ ◊ ◊ ◊ ◊ ◊ ◊ ◊ ◊ ◊ ◊ ◊ ◊ ◊

    c.   script theory. Marvin Minsky and Roger Shank use script theory in AI research.

7.   Victor Hue's study of _____ led to identification of common sounds in spoken words.

a.   script theory

b.   synthesizers

c.   radio waves

d.   spectrograms

◊ ◊ ◊ ◊ ◊ ◊ ◊ ◊ ◊ ◊ ◊ ◊ ◊ ◊ ◊ ◊ ◊ ◊

    d.   spectrograms. The use of spectrograms may change the course of voice-recognition research.

8.   A crucial problem to overcome in robotics is _____ .

a.   vision

b.   touch

c.   mobility

d.   methods of instruction

◊ ◊ ◊ ◊ ◊ ◊ ◊ ◊ ◊ ◊ ◊ ◊ ◊ ◊ ◊ ◊ ◊ ◊

    a.   vision. Presently, a robot's eyes are television cameras that "see" in black and white and in only two dimensions. Unlike humans, they do not judge depth.

9.   People object to universal use of computer-readable cards to control personal financial transactions because they fear that _____ .

a.   the cards will not be accurate

b.   the government will use them to "control" people's behavior

c.   the system will be extremely costly

d.   the cards may be lost or stolen

◊ ◊ ◊ ◊ ◊ ◊ ◊ ◊ ◊ ◊ ◊ ◊ ◊ ◊ ◊ ◊ ◊ ◊ ◊

b. the government will use them to "control" people's behavior. The government would have control over everyone's money and could use its computers to restrict or monitor purchases, possibly to enforce "correct" behavior. The lives of citizens could revolve around the controls placed upon the cards.

10. Demands for on-line database services could decrease if use of _____ increases.
a. books
b. floppy disks
c. optical disks
d. magnetic tape

◊ ◊ ◊ ◊ ◊ ◊ ◊ ◊ ◊ ◊ ◊ ◊ ◊ ◊ ◊ ◊ ◊ ◊ ◊

c. optical disks. Optical disks provide an extremely compact means of storing large volumes of data. Complete databases could be sold inexpensively, thus eliminating the customers' cost of using telecommunications equipment to access information from the databases.

TRUE/FALSE

DIRECTIONS: *Read each question carefully, then circle either T or F to correctly answer each question.*

1. T F As circuits are crowded closer together, the chances increase that one circuit will receive signals from nearby circuits.

2. T F The only reason why microchips are superior to vacuum tubes is that they do not generate any heat.

3. T F Biochips achieve speeds five to seven times that of silicon chips.

4. T F Circuits cannot be damaged by tiny dust particles.

5. T F Today's voice-recognition systems generally have limited vocabularies.

6. T F Voice recognition is best used with short-answer data.

7. T F A voice-controlled robot designed by an engineering laboratory at Stanford University can assist the disabled.

8.   T   F   The Lifecard contains a dedicated computer that performs personal financial transactions.

9.   T   F   Women are more likely than men to become one of the "newly disadvantaged."

10.   T   F   While students are embracing the new skills required to use computers and telecommunications, educators also fear that some old skills will decline.

MATCHING

DIRECTIONS: *Read each question carefully. Choose the correct answer from the list below and write the letter of the answer in the space provided.*

a.   rote learning tool   f.   crosstalk
b.   fiber optics   g.   mathophobia
c.   gallium arsenide chips   h.   multiple processors
d.   biochips   i.   spectrograms
e.   RB5X   j.   associative memory

1.   One advantage to _____ is that they are resistant to radiation.

2.   Since they would be made from living material, _____ could reproduce and repair themselves.

3.   When one circuit on a chip receives unwanted signals from another, this is called _____ .

4.   Light-based processing already is a major factor in _____ links that are replacing copper carriers in the telecommunications field.

5.   A(n) _____ has built-in search capabilities that enable a computer to identify data items on the basis of content.

6.   Computer-enhanced versions of the electrical waveforms of speech are called _____ .

7.   Computer scientists are working diligently on design of operating systems and other software packages that will make it possible to share workloads among _____ .

8.   One of the most complex robots available is the _____ , which comes equipped with ultrasonic and tactile sensors and is available with voice-synthesis equipment and a mechanical arm.

9. Use of computers in schools may help to remove _____ and other fears that may affect normal classroom learning and societal expectations.

10. Teachers in disadvantaged school districts tend to use computers as a _____ .

SHORT ANSWER

DIRECTIONS: *Read each question carefully. Answer each question using three or four complete sentences.*

1. When is heat generation a problem with microchips?

2. How much faster are gallium arsenide chips than standard silicon chips?

3. What is crosstalk?

4.   Why would biochips be able to repair themselves?

5.   What are neural processors? How did they get their name?

6.   What do most of today's computers do best?

7.   What is script theory? How does it concern computers?

8. Why is voice recognition still limited in its uses?

9. How is the National Security Agency using voice-recognition technology?

10. In what areas are existing robots deficient?

ANSWER KEY
True/False

| 1. T | 3. F | 5. T | 7. T | 9. T |

Matching

| 1. c | 3. f | 5. j | 7. h | 9. g |

Short Answer Suggested Responses

Your answers for the odd questions should contain most of the information below.

1.   Chips with high-density packing of circuits generate enough heat to burn themselves out if they are not cooled properly.

3.   Crosstalk occurs when a circuit receives unwanted signals from nearby circuits.

5.   As researchers have attempted to improve the logic processing capabilities of computers for such applications as artificial intelligence, comparisons have been made with the human brain. The brain seems to be able to establish direct links to memory and logic areas through a series of neural paths. Like the human brain, neural processors would be able to select paths in response to the types of problems being processed. The new computers would have considerably more flexibility for establishing data and logic links than present models.

7.   Script theory says that humans have set ideas about how to think in situations they have been through before. Scientists are using script theory in artificial intelligence research, hoping that someday computers might "learn" from experience.

9.   The National Security Agency uses a voice-recognition system to monitor overseas telephone calls. By recognizing key words, NSA's supercomputers can isolate and record suspicious calls.

Section I
Introduction to BASIC

SUMMARY

Using the BASIC programming language will give you an opportunity to work with a computer on a wide variety of tasks. BASIC is an acronym for Beginner's All-Purpose Symbolic Instruction Code. Study of this computer language will help you learn how to manage a computer. This language was developed in the mid-1960s and was originally used with mainframe computers. When the microcomputer came into existence, BASIC was used because of its simplicity and ease of use. This language is considered to be an interactive language and the BASIC statements (or commands) allow you to give instructions to the computer in a conversational manner.

The BASIC language has specific standards (rules) that were established by ANSI (American National Standards Institute). Each computer may have a different version of BASIC, but Microsoft BASIC is the version addressed in this study guide. If you do not have this version of BASIC, you will need to refer to your BASIC programming manual for specific features of your version of BASIC.

A four-step process can serve as a valuable guide in writing computer programs. If you follow this process, you will solve the problem more efficiently and also increase your programming skill. The four steps are (1) define the problem, (2) design a solution, (3) write the program, and (4) submit the program to the computer for testing and debugging.

The first step, defining the problem, involves getting an overview of the problem that needs to be solved. The overview should provide a logical order of the needed processing. There are three parts to the flow of data processing—input, processing, and output. The input part of a program is concerned with entering data into a computer. The processing part performs calculations or manipulates variables. The output part of the program delivers the solution or answer. Answers can be displayed on the screen or printed on paper.

The next step is to design a solution—that is, to develop an algorithm. This step best illustrates the use of structured programming techniques. Structured programming techniques call for the use of top-down design to create a logical and efficient program. This approach enables you to view a program from the general to the specific. Each general task is broken down into smaller and smaller tasks, until each specific task is completed by a BASIC statement. At this point, you should decide how the output will be formatted. By deciding this now, you will save time when you begin to write your program.

Another way to save time when you write your program is to create a structure chart and/or flowchart. With a structure chart, you can identify and organize major program operations into modules. In programming, a module represents the solution to a subproblem. By identifying subproblems during top-down design, you can design and code modules independent of one another.

If you flowchart the problem before you write the program, you can visualize the logical flow of a program. Each symbol stands for a specific step in the program sequence. The flow of the program should start at the top and work toward the bottom. Be aware that a flowchart should have only one starting and one ending point.

The third step is the actual writing (also called coding) of your program. In this step, you will write the actual BASIC statements that will solve your programming problem; if you have planned your program well, this part of the process may be completed in the shortest amount of time.

The fourth or last step is to test and debug your program. This step tests to see if your program will run correctly. If your output has not come out the way you expected, you will have to debug (find and correct) the errors in your program. The debugging process actually begins before the program is entered into the computer. That is, you should visually check the written program for errors before submitting the program. To locate errors that appear during testing, it is recommended that you trace through the program line by line to see where you might have made a mistake.

Most instructions used in BASIC programming fall within two general categories: BASIC statements and BASIC commands. LET, READ, and INPUT are BASIC statements. These statements are assembled into programs to solve specific business, scientific, engineering, and mathematical problems. BASIC commands are used to communicate with the operating system. The most commonly used commands are LIST, NEW, RUN, and SAVE. The LIST command will display a BASIC program that currently is in the computer's main memory. The NEW command instructs the computer to erase any program currently in active memory and prepare for a new program to be entered. The RUN command instructs the computer to execute the program that currently is in main memory. The SAVE command directs the computer to save the program currently in main memory to disk.

STRUCTURED LEARNING

DIRECTIONS: *First, use a blank sheet of paper to cover the answer, without reading it. Then read the question carefully and write the letter of the correct answer in the space provided. Uncover the answer to see if you chose the correct response.*

1. The acronym BASIC stands for _____ .
a. Basic All-Purpose Symbolic Instruction Code
b. Beginner's All-Purpose Symbolic Instruction Code
c. Beginner's All-Symbolic Instruction Code
d. Beginner's All-Purpose Single Instruction Commands

◊ ◊ ◊ ◊ ◊ ◊ ◊ ◊ ◊ ◊ ◊ ◊ ◊ ◊ ◊ ◊ ◊ ◊ ◊

   b.   Beginner's All-Purpose Symbolic Instruction Code. The BASIC language was developed in the mid-1960s to introduce computer novices to programming techniques. BASIC has remained popular because it is easy to learn and to explain.

2. BASIC is considered to be a(n) _____ language.
a. interactive
b. instructional (non-professional)
c. conversational
d. machine-level

◊ ◊ ◊ ◊ ◊ ◊ ◊ ◊ ◊ ◊ ◊ ◊ ◊ ◊ ◊ ◊ ◊ ◊ ◊

   a.   interactive. BASIC is called an interactive language because a programmer can communicate with the computer in response to the execution of program commands. B is an incorrect answer because many professional programmers use BASIC to write programs. D is an incorrect answer because a machine-level language is composed solely of combinations of binary digits—zeroes and ones; BASIC, of course, is composed of easy-to-read, English-like statements and commands.

3. Which of the following refers to top-down, modular design?
a. Under this approach, control of a program only can be transferred downward.
b. This approach cannot be used with the BASIC language.
c. Under this approach, program design begins by studying specific tasks, then proceeds downward to successively more general tasks.
d. Under this approach, a program problem is divided into subproblems that can be solved independently.

◊ ◊ ◊ ◊ ◊ ◊ ◊ ◊ ◊ ◊ ◊ ◊ ◊ ◊ ◊ ◊ ◊ ◊

d.   Under top-down, modular design, a program problem is divided into subproblems that can be solved independently. Top-down design begins by examining the general problem, then identifies more specific, smaller subproblems that can be managed easily and programmed independently.

4.   Which of the following is *not* a BASIC command?
a.   NEW
b.   SAVE
c.   LIST
d.   READ
e.   RUN

◊ ◊ ◊ ◊ ◊ ◊ ◊ ◊ ◊ ◊ ◊ ◊ ◊ ◊ ◊ ◊ ◊ ◊

d.   READ. READ is a BASIC statement that is placed within prgram code. By contrast, BASIC commands are used to communicate with the computer's operating system. Commands are executed immediately when the RETURN or ENTER key is pressed— unless a line number precedes the command.

5.   What function(s) will the NEW command perform?
a.   instructs the computer to be prepared for a new variable name only
b.   directs the computer to execute a program
c.   clears a portion of main memory to prepare for entry of a new program
d.   sets numeric variables to blanks and then executes a program

◊ ◊ ◊ ◊ ◊ ◊ ◊ ◊ ◊ ◊ ◊ ◊ ◊ ◊ ◊ ◊ ◊ ◊

c.   The NEW command clears a portion of main memory to prepare for entry of a new program. When this command is executed, all string variables are given a null value and all numeric variables are given a zero value.

WORKSHEET
1.   Explain the difference between a run-time error and a logic error.

2. Which BASIC commands will cause a program to be executed?

3. Explain one way to visualize the logical flow of a program.

4. Which part of a program focuses on performing calculations or manipulating variables?

5. What design approach encourages the development of a logical, well-organized, and efficient program?

ANSWER KEY
Worksheet

Your answers for the odd worksheet questions should contain most of the information below. Questions requiring specific responses should match the answers given below.

1. A run-time error occurs when the computer is unable to execute a program or a portion of a program. A logic error, on the other hand, occurs when the computer is able to execute the program, but processing leads to unexpected and undesirable output.

3. One way to visualize the logical flow of a program is to create or study a flowchart of program operations. On a flowchart, the logical flow of data and program instructions are displayed through the use of graphic symbols and brief descriptions contained within the symbols. A flowchart should have only one starting point and one end point.

5. Top-down, modular design is a problem-solving approach in which a problem is studied first at its most general level. Then the overall problem is divided into smaller, more specific problems that can be understood and solved independently. A solution to a subproblem is called a module. This top-down division of general problems into successively more specific subproblems continues until all tasks can be expressed with programming-language statements.

Section II
Getting Started With BASIC

SUMMARY

This section discusses some of the components of the BASIC language: line numbers, constants, character strings, and variables. In addition, the elementary BASIC statements REM, LET, PRINT, and END are discussed.

The first component, line numbers, specifies whether a line will be executed in direct or indirect mode. If a BASIC statement has line numbers, it is in the indirect mode. This means the statements will not execute until the RUN command is given. If line numbers are not present, the BASIC statements are considered to be in the direct mode, in which case each BASIC statement is executed as soon as the <RETURN> or <ENTER> key is pressed. Also, in the direct mode the statements are not placed in main memory. This means that a statement in the direct mode will have to be typed in each time you would like it to execute.

Once you have decided whether or not line numbers are to be used, your next decision will be to identify constants and variables. Constants are divided into numeric constants and character string constants. Numeric constants are numbers. Character string constants are alphanumeric values that may consist of letters and numbers and are surrounded by quotation marks. Remember, constants will not change during the execution of the program.

Variables are storage locations, the values of which may change during execution. There are two types of variables: the numeric type and string variables. A numeric variable may hold numbers, while a string variable may only hold string values. String values are alphanumeric data enclosed in quotation marks. Numeric values are not enclosed in quotation marks.

Within BASIC statements, you should not use reserved words in your variable names. Reserved words are specific to each machine and there usually is a table that will list the words you cannot use as variable names. In fact, some versions of BASIC do not allow you to embed the reserved words within a variable name either. Check with your BASIC manual to see how particular your specific version is.

The first of the elementary BASIC statements is REM. The primary function of this statement is to document a program. This statement can be placed anywhere in a program and should be used frequently. REM statements are not only for the programmer who wrote the program, but also for anyone who might read the program later. While remarks lines are non-executable, which means that the computer ignores them, these statements can be invaluable for making a program more readable.

The LET statement assigns values to variables. Values stored by LET statements are placed in memory locations. These variable names are names for the memory locations within the computer. When placing values in variables, you should make sure that you match numeric values with numeric variables, and string values with string variables. Be aware that numeric data placed in a string variable must be enclosed in quotation marks. If numbers are placed in a string variable, they cannot be used in arithmetic expressions.

Arithmetic expressions can consist of constants, numeric variables, and arithmetic operators. Arithmetic operators are the symbols that show what operation should be performed. These operators consist of the addition, subtraction, multiplication, division, exponentiation, and parentheses symbols. When an arithmetic expression has more than one operation to perform, a specific hierarchy will be followed.

In this sense, a hierarchy is the order, or priority, in which each of the operations will be completed. The parentheses are considered first, then exponentiation, multiplication and division, and, finally, addition and subtraction. If one of the levels is not present, the following level is performed. If two or more operations are on the same priority level, they are performed from left to right.

The PRINT statement is responsible for the form in which the output of a program is displayed or printed.

To print the value of a variable, you specify the variable name to be printed.

To print character string literals—expressions of alphabetic, numeric, or special characters—you place them in quotation marks. While the literal is on the right side of the equal sign, the variable name would be on the left side. To print out a numeric literal, you simply specify the number. Remember that, while character string literals need quotation marks, numeric literals do not.

To print a blank line, you use the word PRINT. You also may specify the number of blank lines you would like by coding that many PRINT statements.

The END statement usually is the last statement in a program and should have all nines for a line number. Using all nines can help you identify the location of the END statement easily. In turn, easy visual identification of an END statement can prevent you from ending a program prematurely by misplacing the statment.

STRUCTURED LEARNING

DIRECTIONS: *First, use a blank sheet of paper to cover the answer, without reading it. Then read the question carefully and write the letter of the correct answer in the space provided. Uncover the answer to see if you chose the correct response.*

1.   Which of the following is a variable type?
a.   processing
b.   elementary
c.   numeric
d.   sequential

◊ ◊ ◊ ◊ ◊ ◊ ◊ ◊ ◊ ◊ ◊ ◊ ◊ ◊ ◊ ◊ ◊ ◊ ◊

   c.   numeric. A numeric variable is a valid variable type. Two general types of variables are available to BASIC programmers: numeric and string.

2.   In executing a BASIC program, the indirect mode occurs in what situation?
a.   When each BASIC statement is preceded by a line number.
b.   When the computer is operating in high-resolution graphics mode.
c.   Only when all BASIC statements are not preceded by line numbers.
d.   When BASIC statements are not arranged in sequential order.

◊ ◊ ◊ ◊ ◊ ◊ ◊ ◊ ◊ ◊ ◊ ◊ ◊ ◊ ◊ ◊ ◊ ◊ ◊

   a.   The indirect mode of program execution takes place when each BASIC statement is preceded by a line number. The RUN command must be used to execute a program in indirect mode.

3.   Which of the following is *not* a BASIC statement?
a.   REM
b.   PRINT
c.   END
d.   CONSTANT

◊ ◊ ◊ ◊ ◊ ◊ ◊ ◊ ◊ ◊ ◊ ◊ ◊ ◊ ◊ ◊ ◊ ◊ ◊

   d.   CONSTANT. A CONSTANT is not a BASIC statement. It is a general programming term that refers to a value that cannot change during program execution.

4.   Which of the following statements is used to place comments in a program?

a.   COMM

b.   REMARK

c.   REM

d.   COMMENT

◊ ◊ ◊ ◊ ◊ ◊ ◊ ◊ ◊ ◊ ◊ ◊ ◊ ◊ ◊ ◊ ◊ ◊

    d.   REM. In BASIC, you use the REM statement to specify that a line contains a comment, rather than an executable program statement. The computer will ignore REM statements when it executes a BASIC program. A REM statement can be placed anywhere within a program.

5.   What function(s) will the END statement perform?

a.   instructs the computer to quit accepting variable names

b.   causes program execution to stop

c.   causes program control to be passed to the first statement in the program

d.   specifies that printing or display of information is to stop

◊ ◊ ◊ ◊ ◊ ◊ ◊ ◊ ◊ ◊ ◊ ◊ ◊ ◊ ◊ ◊ ◊ ◊

    b.   The END statement represents the logical end of a program and causes program execution to stop. BASIC programmers frequently precede the END statement with a line number of all nines.

WORKSHEET

1.   What will the REM statement do in the following program segment?

```
10  REM LET X = 0
20  LET Y = 3
30  LET X = Y
40  PRINT Y
```

2.   What will be printed when this program segment is entered at the keyboard?

           10 LET X = 10
           20 PRINT X
           30 PRINT X + 5

3.   Which of the following lines of BASIC are in the correct format? Explain why the other lines are incorrect.

a.   LET LET X = 10

b.   10 REM LET Y + X = A

c.   PRINT NAME,A$,T1

d.   20 PRINT NA3;ADDRESS,7Y

e.   10 LET A = Y

f.   10 PRINT The answers to the problem are 10, 20, 30."

g.   30 PRINT "A$";" and B$";" are equal to ";C$

h.   30 REM "The next program module performs the calculations.

4.   Which line number will cause the following program to stop its execution?

        10 REM *** THIS IS A TEST PROGRAM ***
        20 LET A = 2
        30 LET B = 3
        40 REM END
        50 LET C = A + B
        60 PRINT C
        70 END

5.   Convert the following numbers from scientific notation to decimal numbers.

a.   7.324E06
b.   -2.58E03
c.   9.991E-04
d.   3.7294E+05

6. What would be the output from the following programming segment?

```
10  REM *** THE FOLLOWING PROGRAM WILL PRINT ***
20  REM *** THE NAMES OF A SPECIFIED NUMBER OF ***
30  REM *** PEOPLE. ***
35  REM
40  LET A = 0
50  LET A = A + 1
60  LET N1AME$ = "RYAN"
70  LET N2AME$ = "NORMA"
80  PRINT N2AME$;" and ";N1AME$;" are the names of two
    people."
99  END
```

7. Which of the following are not valid examples of character strings?
Why are they not valid?

a.   10 LET A$ = "352-1395"

b.   10 LET TOTAL$ = $130000

c.   10 LT$ = "1616 Napoleon Road"

d.   10 LET FF$ = "BRUCE SPRINGSTEEN

e.   10 LET PHIL$ = "NO JACKET REQUIRED"

f.   10 LET ANSWER$ = "200,000"

8. Which of the following are numeric variable names and which are character string variable names?
   a. A123$
   b. STATE
   c. N1AME$
   d. PEOPLE1$
   e. RR12
   f. K46$

9. Write the value of each of the following numeric variables.
   a. 30 LET X = 4 * (5 + 3) / 2 - 3
   b. 30 LET A12 = ((4 / 2 - 1) + 3) * 2
   c. 30 LET R = 12 * 3 / 4 + (7 - 3)
   d. 30 LET Y4 = 6 / 2 * 3 + 9 -2

10. Write a BASIC statement that will perform each of the following functions.

a. Print the sentence "BASIC programming is enjoyable."
    (Also print the quotation marks.)

b. Write a line of code that will terminate a program.

c. Print a blank line.

d. Display a comment within a program.

e. Print the number 2,345,600.

f. Print the equation: 120 + 123000 = 123120.

PROGRAMMING PROBLEM 1

Your astronomy professor would like you to print the names of the planets in our solar system. Make certain you print the planet names in a column. Also print them beginning with the planet closest to the sun, then preceding outward through the solar system. This program should be documented properly, which means that REM statements should be used to describe the program as well as the functions of modules.

The program output should appear in this format:

THE PLANETS WITHIN OUR SOLAR SYSTEM
—————————————————————————————
MERCURY
XXXXXX
XXXXXX

To refresh your astronomical knowledge, the planets in the solar system are Mercury, Venus, Earth, Mars, Jupiter, Saturn, Uranus, Neptune, and Pluto.

PROGRAMMING PROBLEM 1 (cont.)

PROGRAMMING PROBLEM 2

Frederick Johnson has just purchased a fish farm and a new computer. This type of fish farm will produce trout for the general public as well as for sport fishing. In an effort to plan the amount of trout that will be available during the upcoming season and to use his computer fully, he has decided to calculate how many trout he will harvest this season and how much money he will make. Johnson has an estimated 12,000 trout. He estimates that 4,500 mature trout, weighing an average of three pounds, will be ready for harvesting by the start of the season. A trout weighing three pounds or more will yield $2.99 per pound at the market.

Johnson would like his report to list the number of estimated mature trout, the total of estimated pounds of trout he expects to harvest, and the amount of money he will earn.

The output should look similar to this:

```
FREDERICK JOHNSON'S TROUT FARM
——————————————————————
ESTIMATED NUMBER OF MATURE
      TROUT (APPROXIMATELY 3 POUNDS)    XXXXX
TOTAL ESTIMATED POUNDS OF
      HARVESTABLE TROUT                 XXXXX
—————————————————————————————————
      ESTIMATED REVENUE                 XXXXX
```

PROGRAMMING PROBLEM 2 (cont.)

ANSWER KEY
Worksheet

Your answers for the odd worksheet questions should contain most of the information below. Questions requiring specific responses should match the answers given below.

1. The REM statement indicates a comment within a program, and does not specify an executable statement. Thus, the computer will ignore the REM statement in this program.

3. Lines that contain correct code are b, e, g, and h. Lines for both a and c have a missing line number. The line for d is in error because 7Y is an incorrectly formatted variable name. All variable names must begin with a letter of the alphabet. The line for f is missing a quotation mark. All character strings must be enclosed within quotation marks, although variable names do not need quotation marks.

5. a.   7,324,000
    b.   -2,580
    c.   .0009991
    d.   .372,940

7. The incorrect character strings are b and d. Answer b is incorrect because the character string is not enclosed within quotation marks. For Answer d, the character string is missing an ending quotation mark.

9. a.   X = 13
    b.   A12 = 8
    c.   R = 13
    d.   Y4 = 16

Solution to Programming Problem 1

```
10     REM ***                    SPACESHIP TO THE STARS                      ***
20     REM
30     REM *** THIS PROGRAM WILL PRINT THE PLANETS THAT ARE IN OUR   ***
40     REM *** SOLAR SYSTEM.  THE LIST WILL START AT THE CLOSEST      ***
50     REM *** PLANET, MERCURY, AND WORK OUTWARDS TO THE PLANET       ***
60     REM *** PLUTO.                                                 ***
65     REM
70     REM *** MAJOR VARIABLES:
80     REM ***                    P#LANET$        REPRESENTS THE PLANETS     ***
90     REM
100    REM  1.0 ASSIGN VALUES TO VARIABLES
110    REM
120         LET P1LANET$ = "MERCURY"
130         LET P2LANET$ = "VENUS"
140         LET P3LANET$ = "EARTH"
150         LET P4LANET$ = "MARS"
160         LET P5LANET$ = "JUPITER"
170         LET P6LANET$ = "SATURN"
180         LET P7LANET$ = "URANUS"
190         LET P8LANET$ = "NEPTUNE"
200         LET P9LANET$ = "PLUTO"
210    REM
220    REM  2.0 PRINT HEADING AND PLANET NAMES
230    REM
240         PRINT "THE PLANETS WITHIN THE SOLAR SYSTEM"
250         PRINT "-----------------------------------
260         PRINT
270         PRINT P1LANET$
280         PRINT P2LANET$
290         PRINT P3LANET$
300         PRINT P4LANET$
310         PRINT P5LANET$
320         PRINT P6LANET$
330         PRINT P7LANET$
340         PRINT P8LANET$
350         PRINT P9LANET$
360         PRINT
999    END
```

```
RUN
THE PLANETS WITHIN THE SOLAR SYSTEM
-----------------------------------

MERCURY
VENUS
EARTH
MARS
JUPITER
SATURN
URANUS
NEPTUNE
PLUTO
```

Section III
Input and Output

SUMMARY

This section discusses two ways to enter data to a program. One way uses the INPUT statement; the second uses a combination of the READ and DATA statements. The final part of this section explains the methods of structuring the output of a program with PRINT statements.

The INPUT statement allows you to enter data to a program inter-actively, typically through a question-and-response format. At the point when you need some information entered, it is recommended that you use a prompt. When an INPUT statement executes, it displays only a question mark, unless a prompt is included. This prompt (or message) should indicate what data are being requested by the program. With a long program, if you do not use a prompt, you may not remember what type of data the program is requesting.

The INPUT statement will allow you to enter more than one value at a time; in addition, the values may be of different types. This means you may enter numeric and character data at the same time. Data values are separated by commas. If you do not enter enough data values, the computer will continue to display the question mark until the correct number and type of data are entered.

While you may use a PRINT statement as a prompt, it also is possible to have the prompt included in the INPUT statement. The prompt should describe the type of data needed.

When a prompt is to be displayed, you may want to clear the screen so that the user can see the prompt clearly. The CLS statement will perform this function for you. It clears the whole screen and then places the cursor in the upper-left corner. Once this is accomplished, you can place your prompt anywhere on the screen. Be aware that each type of computer may handle this situation differently, so check your user's manual for details.

Another way data can be entered to a program is through the READ and DATA statements. The READ/DATA statements are different from the INPUT statement because you decide what values will be needed before the execution of the program. When the program initially is executed, all the values in the DATA statements are placed into a data list. This list takes the values in order of DATA statements from left to right. The values are not sorted, so it is important that you have the values in the correct order. If you should mix up the data values, the program may attempt to assign a character string to a real variable, causing program execution to stop prematurely.

When the READ/DATA and INPUT statements are used to enter data, the PRINT statement is used to display the output of a program. When you use the PRINT statement, you can specify the exact format of program output. You can accomplish this formatting by using commas or semicolons, which have specific meanings to the computer.

The comma will display output in a specific print zone. Microsoft BASIC has 5.7 print zones, with each print zone being 14 characters wide. The first zone starts in column one, the second zone begins in column 15. By separating the items in a PRINT statement, you can make your output easy to read. If the printed value exceeds the print zone, following commas will cause printing to begin in the next unused zone. If a comma appears after the last item in a PRINT statement, the printing will continue into the next zone.

STRUCTURED LEARNING

DIRECTIONS: *First, use a blank sheet of paper to cover the answer, without reading it. Then read the question carefully and write the letter of the correct answer in the space provided. Uncover the answer to see if you chose the correct response.*

1.   Which BASIC statement is used to enter data when a program asks a question and waits for a user response?
a.   INTERACTIVE
b.   INPUT
c.   ASSIGNMENT
d.   READ/DATA

◊ ◊ ◊ ◊ ◊ ◊ ◊ ◊ ◊ ◊ ◊ ◊ ◊ ◊ ◊ ◊ ◊ ◊

b.   INPUT. The INPUT statement is used to support an interactive, question-and-response program execution. With INPUT, the user can enter data into a program while the program is running. Data items are entered by the user through the keyboard, in response to program prompts.

2.   What is an INPUT variable list?
a.   A list of variable names that may be used in a program.
b.   A list that places values into an INPUT statement each time a loop is executed.

c.   A sequence of variables, separated by commas, that specifies data values required by a program for processing

d.   A list that causes the values of variables to be printed.

◊ ◊ ◊ ◊ ◊ ◊ ◊ ◊ ◊ ◊ ◊ ◊ ◊ ◊ ◊ ◊ ◊ ◊ ◊

c.   An INPUT variable list is a sequence of variables, with each variable separated from others by commas, that specifies the data values required by a program. When a program reaches an INPUT statement, it stops and waits for the user to enter the data values, in the correct order.

3. What does the CLS instruction do?

a.   Closes a file and makes it impossible for a program to reuse that file until an OPEN statement is encountered.

b.   Copies data values into the correct variables.

c.   Executes the Cursor Linear Sequence, which aids the monitor in scanning all lines of the screen correctly.

d.   Clears the screen and places the cursor in the upper left-hand corner of the screen.

◊ ◊ ◊ ◊ ◊ ◊ ◊ ◊ ◊ ◊ ◊ ◊ ◊ ◊ ◊ ◊ ◊ ◊ ◊

d.   The CLS statement performs two functions: clearing the screen and placing the cursor in the upper-left corner of the screen. This statement is beneficial when you want existing screen information to be removed before program output is displayed.

4. Which of the following statements enters data to a program without using the INPUT statement?

a.   PUT/GET

b.   READ/LIST, which can be used to enter large amounts of data

c.   READ/DATA, which assign values to variables as the program executes

d.   the DATA step statement, which assigns values to variable names

◊ ◊ ◊ ◊ ◊ ◊ ◊ ◊ ◊ ◊ ◊ ◊ ◊ ◊ ◊ ◊ ◊ ◊ ◊

c.   The two statements READ/DATA are used in combination to assign predetermined values to variables while the program executes. This is a convenient way to enter large amounts of data to a program without the need for an input operator to be present and without the need for interactive prompts and responses.

5. Which of the following punctuation marks is used in the PRINT statement to specify printing to begin in the next avaiable print zone?

a. asterisk

b. period

c. leading spaces

d. comma

◊ ◊ ◊ ◊ ◊ ◊ ◊ ◊ ◊ ◊ ◊ ◊ ◊ ◊ ◊ ◊ ◊ ◊

    d.   comma. You can use a comma to specify the print zone in which you would like printing to begin.

WORKSHEET

1. Write two INPUT statements— one to replace the lines of code in (a) below, and another to replace the lines of code (b) below.

a.   10 PRINT "ENTER YOUR NAME"
     20 INPUT N$

b.   10 PRINT "ENTER DESTINATION AND THE DISTANCE IN MILES"
     20 INPUT D$,M

2. Which of the following program segments are invalid? Why?

a.   10 PRINT "WHAT DAY DO YOU RIDE THE BUS?"
     20 INPUT "DAY$"

b.   10 INPUT "WHAT IS THE COST OF THE AIRPLANE PART?";CST

c.   10 PRINT "THE NEXT EXIT WILL BE WHAT?"
     20 INPUT EXIT$

d.   10 INPUT PRINT "THE NEXT NUMBER IN THE SEQUENCE IS";NUM

e.   20 INPUT MONTH$
     30 INPUT "ENTER BOOK TITLE ";TITLE$

3. Which of the following program segments will accept these data values in the order given?

          STATE$ = "OHIO"
          COLLEGE$ = "BALDWIN WALLACE"
          EXPENSE$ = "3,000"

a.   10 PRINT "ENTER STATE,COLLEGE,EXPENSES"
     20 INPUT COLLEGE$;STATE;EXPENSE$

b.   10 PRINT "ENTER STATE,COLLEGE,EXPENSES"
     20 INPUT STATE$,COLLEGE$;EXPENSE

c.   10 PRINT "ENTER STATE,COLLEGE,EXPENSES"
     20 INPUT STATE$,COLLEGE$,EXPENSE$

d.   10 PRINT "ENTER STATE,COLLEGE,EXPENSES"
     20 INPUT STATE$,COLLEGE$
     30 INPUT EXPENSE

4. Which of the following READ statements would cause an error when
    this DATA statement is used?

    10 DATA 10,25,356,"TIME",56,"75.00"

a. 50 READ A,H1,JOB1
b. 10 READ E34,TT,U12,G$,E3
c. 100 READ TY2,D6,Y,K8,EX9,H$
d. 15 READ XE,T16,P123,K8$,C8,H$

Use the following program segment to answer Questions 5 and 6:

    10 LET X$ = "JONATHON"
    20 READ A,WE$
    30 DATA 2,"JAMES",3,"YOLANDA","KAYLENE"
    40 READ A,WE$,X$
    50 PRINT A,WE$,X$

5. What will occur when line 20 is executed?

6. What will happen when lines 40 and 50 are executed?

7. Suppose the values 2500, 3500, 4500 must be stored in the variables P1, P2, and P3, respectively. Show three different ways this can be done (by using the LET, READ, and INPUT statements).

8. What will be the output from the following program?

```
10 READ J,A,N$
20 LET C = J * A
30 PRINT J,"$";C
40 PRINT N$
50 DATA 40,10,"JOHN LENNON"
```

9. Write a PRINT statement that will output the following lines.

	Print Zone 1	Print Zone 2	Print Zone 3
a.	THOMAS WATSON		
b.	1	3	5
c.	A	BC	DEF
d.	EMILY DICKINSON'S		POEMS

10. What output will be generated from each of the following PRINT statements?

a.   20 PRINT,"TIME TO LEAVE THIS TOWN, MARSHALL."

b.   20 PRINT,"MIKE";"&";"JEFF ARE";"GEOLOGISTS

c.   20 PRINT,,"PRINT",,

d.   20 PRINT "TIME","WILL","ONLY","TELL."

PROGRAMMING PROBLEM 1

Victor's Video, Inc. currently exports top-of-the-line, U.S.-made video-phones and satellite dishes. The company would like a program that prints a breakdown of shipments by country. The program outputs the country to which products are shipped, followed by the number of videophones and satellite dishes purchased, the total amount of the sale, and the current date of the report.

Data to be input to this program are:

List Price: VideoPhone I— $ 650
                 VideoPhone II— $ 800
                 Sa-tell2 (rooftop version)— $1400
                 All-tellx (backyard version)— $6500

Use READ/DATA statements to input the prices of these products.

Run this program using the current date. Sales for a test country will be for Japan— 120 VideoPhone II, two Sa-tell2, and three All-tellx. Use INPUT statements to enter the curent date and the number of products shipped. The output should look similar to the following:

```
        VICTOR'S VIDEO, INC.
        ---------------                    DATE: XX/XX/XX


     COUNTRY SHIPPED TO: .XXXXXXXXXXXXXXX

     NUMBER OF PRODUCTS SHIPPED:

     VideoPhone I                  XXXX
     VideoPhone II                 XXXX
     Sa-tell2 (rooftop version)    XXXX
     All-tellx (backyard version)  XXXX

     TOTAL AMOUNT OF SALE = $XXXXXX
```

PROGRAMMING PROBLEM 1 (cont.)

PROGRAMMING PROBLEM 2

The J & M Geological Survey Company wants to track sales of its oil maps. These maps are used by oil companies to aid in deciding where to locate new oil drilling rigs. These maps show whether conditions are favorable for oil in a particular region. The oil companies then can study the maps to decide whether to buy mineral rights for specific plots of land.

Three different types of maps can be purchased from J & M, and each type of map provides different information. Map types are Beginning Explorer, Intermediate Land Parcels, and Expert Geologist.

Jeff and Mike, the owners of J & M Geological Survey Company, would like a report that outputs daily unit sales for the three map types. The unit prices for the maps are: Beginning Explorer— $125, Intermediate Land Parcels— $275, Expert Geologist— $375. Use READ/DATA statements to input the prices of these maps.

Execute this program using the current date and the following sales data:

Beginning Explorer— 55
Intermediate Land Parcels— 175
Expert Geologist— 75

Use INPUT statements to enter the current date and the sales for each day. The output should appear similar to the following:

J & M GEOLOGICAL SURVEY COMPANY
—————————————————————————————

NAME OF MAP	NUMBER SOLD	DOLLAR SALES
BEGINNING EXPLORER	55	$XXXX
INTERMEDIATE LAND PARCELS	175	$XXXX
EXPERT GEOLOGIST	75	$XXXX

TOTAL SALES = $XXXXXX

PROGRAMMING PROBLEM 2 (cont.)

ANSWER KEY

Your answers for the odd worksheet questions should contain most of the information below. Questions requiring specific responses should match the answers given below.

Worksheet

1.　a.　10 INPUT "ENTER YOUR NAME";N$

　　b.　10 INPUT "ENTER DESTINATION AND THE DISTANCE IN MILES";"D$,M

3.　Answer (c) is in the correct format to accept the specified data values.

　　10 PRINT "ENTER STATE,COLLEGE,EXPENSES"
　　20 INPUT STATE$,COLLEGE$,EXPENSE$

5.　The READ statement would accept the first two values in the DATA statement and place them in ther respective variables. Thus, the value 2 would be assigned to A, and the value JAMES would be assigned to WE$.

7.　LET statements:

　　10 LET P1 = 2500
　　20 LET P2 = 3500
　　30 LET P3 = 4500

　　READ statement:

　　10 READ P1,P2,P3
　　20 DATA 2500,3500,4500

　　INPUT statement:

　　10 PRINT "ENTER THE VALUES FOR P1, P2, P3"
　　20 INPUT P1,P2,P3

9.　a.　10 PRINT "THOMAS WATSON"

　　b.　10 PRINT "1","3","5"

　　c.　10 PRINT "A","BC","DEF"

　　d.　10 PRINT EMILY DICKINSON'S","POEMS"

Solution to Programming Problem 1

```
10      REM ***                  SATELLITE SUMMARY                      ***
20      REM
30      REM *** THIS REPORT WILL SUMMARIZE THE TOTAL AMOUNT OF THE SALE ***
40      REM *** OF EACH PRODUCT SHIPPED TO A SPECIFIC COUNTRY.   THE    ***
50      REM *** REPORT WILL THEN SUMMARIZE THE TOTAL AMOUNT OF THE SALE. ***
55      REM
60      REM *** MAJOR VARIABLES:                                        ***
70      REM ***          V1DEO$, V2DEO$, S1ATEL$, S2ATEL$  (PRODUCTS)   ***
80      REM ***          P1, P2, R1, R2                    (PRICES)     ***
90      REM
100     REM               1.1 READ PRODUCT PRICES
105     REM
110         READ V1DEO$,P1,V2DEO$,P2
120         READ S1ATEL$,R1,S2ATEL$,R2
130         CLS
140     REM
150     REM               1.2 ENTER TODAY'S DATE
155     REM
160         PRINT
170         INPUT "ENTER TODAY'S DATE   ",CURDAT$
180         PRINT
190     REM
200     REM               2.1 INPUT COUNTRY NAME
205     REM
210         INPUT "ENTER THE NAME OF THE COUNTRY YOU ARE SHIPPING TO:  " INPT$
212         PRINT
215     REM
220     REM               2.2 ENTER AMOUNTS OF EACH PRODUCT SHIPPED
225     REM
230         INPUT "HOW MANY VIDEOPHONE-I WERE SHIPPED?  ",A1MT
240         PRINT
250         LET T1TLVID = A1MT * P1
260         INPUT "HOW MANY VIDEOPHONE-II WERE SHIPPED?  ",A2MT
270         PRINT
280         LET T2TLVID = A2MT * P2
290         INPUT "HOW MANY SA-TELL2 WERE SHIPPED?  ",S1TELL
300         PRINT
310         LET SATT = S1TELL * R1
320         INPUT "HOW MANY ALL-TELLX WERE SHIPPED?  ",S2TELL
330         PRINT
340         LET S2ATT = S2TELL * R2
350         LET SALES = T1TLVID + T2TLVID + SATT + S2ATT
360     REM
370     REM               3.0 PRINT HEADING AND PRODUCTS SOLD TO EACH COUNTRY
380     REM
390         CLS
400         PRINT
410         PRINT
420         PRINT ,,"VICTOR'S VIDEO, INC."
430         PRINT ,,"--------------------",
440         PRINT "DATE:  ";CURDAT$
450         PRINT
460         PRINT "COUNTRY SHIPPED TO:  ";INPT$
470         PRINT
480         PRINT "NUMBER OF PRODUCTS SHIPPED:"
490         PRINT "--------------------------"
500         PRINT
510         PRINT V1DEO$,,A1MT
520         PRINT V2DEO$,,A2MT
530         PRINT S1ATEL$,,S1TELL
540         PRINT S2ATEL$,,S2TELL
550         PRINT
560         PRINT "TOTAL AMOUNT OF SALE = $";SALES
570     REM
580     REM               4.0 DATA STATEMENTS
585
590         DATA "VIDEOPHONE-I",650,"VIDEOPHONE-II",800
600         DATA "SA-TELL2",1400,"ALL-TELLX",6500
999     END
```

Solution to Programming Problem 1 (cont.)

```
ENTER TODAY'S DATE  3/5/90

ENTER THE NAME OF THE COUNTRY YOU ARE SHIPPING TO:  JAPAN

HOW MANY VIDEOPHONE-I WERE SHIPPED?  0

HOW MANY VIDEOPHONE-II WERE SHIPPED?  120

HOW MANY SA-TELL2 WERE SHIPPED?  2

HOW MANY ALL-TELLX WERE SHIPPED?  3


                        VICTOR'S VIDEO, INC.
                        --------------------        DATE:  3/5/90

COUNTRY SHIPPED TO:  JAPAN

NUMBER OF PRODUCTS SHIPPED:
--------------------------

VIDEOPHONE-I                    0
VIDEOPPHONE-II                  120
SA-TELL2                        2
ALL-TELLX                       3

TOTAL AMOUNT OF SALE = $ 118300
```

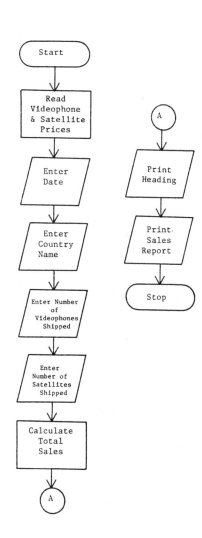

Section IV
Looping

SUMMARY

The FOR/NEXT statements and WHILE/WEND are two types of loops.

The FOR/NEXT loop is very useful in programs for which the exact number of loop repetitions is known before the loop is executed; therefore, it is referred to as a counting loop.

The FOR statement defines how many times the loop is to be executed. The loop control variable is first set to an initial value. This value is tested against the terminal value each time the statement is executed to determine whether to continue the loop or direct execution to the line immediately after the NEXT statement. The step value specifies the amount to be added to the loop control variable at the end of each loop repetition. If the step value is omitted from the FOR statement, +1 will be added automatically to the loop control variable.

The NEXT statement increments the loop control variable by the amount of the step value. It also compares the loop control variable with the terminal value; if it is less than or equal to the loop control variable, the loop is executed again.

The following rules apply to the use of FOR/NEXT statements.

1. A negative step value may be used. If used, the initial value must be greater than the terminal value in order for the loop to execute.

2. The step value never should be zero; doing this will create an infinite loop.

3. Transfer can be made from one statement to another within a loop but never from within the loop to the FOR statement.

4. The value of the loop control variable should not be modified by statements within the loop.

5. The initial, terminal, and step expressions can be composed of any valid numeric variable, constant, or mathematical formula.

6. Each FOR statement must be accompanied by an associated NEXT statement that contains the same loop control variable.

The WHILE/WEND loop is used when, prior to entering the loop, it is not known how many times a loop will have to be executed. When the WHILE/WEND loop is used, the loop control variable is not automatically set to an initial value; therefore, it must be initialized before the WHILE statement is encountered.

The WHILE statement evaluates the expression as either true or false. The body of the loop is executed until the WEND statement is encountered, only if the expression evaluates as true. Otherwise, control is transferred to the first statement following the WEND. When the WEND statement is encountered (notice that there is no variable following the WEND), control is passed back to the WHILE statement and the expression is evaluated once again. The loop control variable is not automatically altered during the loop repetition as it is during the FOR/NEXT loop; therefore, this task must be performed by the program itself.

The expression of the WHILE statement can be used to compare the loop control variables with a trailer value, which is a dummy value that marks the end of the input data. The trailer value can be either a numeric value or a character string, depending on the type of loop control variable being used, but it must always be a value outside of the range of the actual loop control variable data.

STRUCTURED LEARNING

DIRECTIONS: *First, use a blank sheet of paper to cover the answer, without reading it. Then read the question carefully and write the letter of the correct answer in the space provided. Uncover the answer to see if you chose the correct response.*

1. When FOR/NEXT statements are used to code a loop, the variable whose value is to be changed each time the loop is executed appears in _____ .
   a. only the FOR statement
   b. a REM statement preceding the loop
   c. only the NEXT statement
   d. both the FOR and NEXT statements

◊ ◊ ◊ ◊ ◊ ◊ ◊ ◊ ◊ ◊ ◊ ◊ ◊ ◊ ◊ ◊ ◊ ◊

   d. The variable is specified in both the FOR and NEXT statements. Here is an example:

```
10 FOR I = 1 TO 5
   .
   .
   .
40 NEXT I
```

When the FOR statement is executed the first time, it sets the loop control variable I to 1 (the indicated initial value) and tests to see if the value I has exceeded the indicated terminal value (5, in this case). When the NEXT statement is executed, the computer adds the step value (+1, in this case) to the value of the loop control variable, and returns control to the top of the loop.

2.   The step size used in a FOR statement _____ .
a.   is always one
b.   is always positive
c.   cannot be negative
d.   cannot be zero

    d.   cannot be zero. The number following the word STEP tells the computer the value by which the loop control variable should be incremented each time the loop is executed. If the step clause is omitted, the step value is assumed to be +1. The step value also can be negative. However, the step size should never be zero; this would cause the computer to execute the loop an endless number of times (an infinite loop).

3.   Which two of the following are techniques for loop control?
a.   trailer value
b.   the LET statement
c.   counters
d.   the END statement

    a and c. A loop controlled by a trailer value contains a relational operator that checks for a value that signifies the end of data. The counter is incremented each time the loop is executed; the loop ends when the expression controlling loop repetition becomes false.

4.   Which of the following does *not* occur when a WHILE/WEND loop is executed?
a.   The statements in the loop are executed if the expression evaluates as true.
b.   The initial value must be set before the WHILE statement is executed for the first time.

c. The loop control variable is incremented or decremented automatically.

d. Each time the WEND statement is encountered the value of the loop control variable is tested to see if the condition still is true.

◊ ◊ ◊ ◊ ◊ ◊ ◊ ◊ ◊ ◊ ◊ ◊ ◊ ◊ ◊ ◊ ◊ ◊

c. The loop control variable is not automaticaly set to an initial value, nor is it automatically altered during each loop repetition. Therefore, these tasks must be performed by the program.

5. What will the following module print when it is executed?

```
10 LET A = 2
20 WHILE A <> 4
30      FOR I = 3 TO 1 STEP -2
40          PRINT I * A,
50          A = A + 1
60      NEXT I
70      PRINT
80 WEND
99 END
```

a. 6   2
    9   3

b. 6   2   9   3   12   4

c. 6   2
    9   3
    12   4

d. 6
    2
    9
    3

◊ ◊ ◊ ◊ ◊ ◊ ◊ ◊ ◊ ◊ ◊ ◊ ◊ ◊ ◊ ◊ ◊ ◊

a. The initial value of the loop control variable is 3 and is decreased by 2 each time the loop is executed until the variable is less than 1. Thus, I will equal 3 and 1 during the execution of the FOR loop. A is initially equal to 2, so PRINT I * A will cause 6 and 2 to be printed on the same line, but in separate print zones. Then, A is incremented to 3 and the WHILE expression evaluates as true. In response, the FOR loop executes again, causing 9 and 3 to be printed on the same line, in separate print zones. When A is incremented the second time it equals 4, which causes the WHILE expression to evaluate as false. Thus, program execution stops.

WORKSHEET

1. What output will be provided for each of the following program segments?

a. ```
    10 FOR J = 5 TO 15 STEP 5
    20   PRINT J * 2,
    30 NEXT J
    40 PRINT "THAT'S ALL"
    99 END
    ```

b.  ```
    10 FOR L = 6 TO 18 STEP 3
    20          PRINT "$*";
    30 NEXT L
    99
    ```

c. ```
    10 FOR N = 6 TO 1 STEP -1
    20   PRINT N
    30 NEXT N
    99 END
    ```

2.  Identify the loop control variable, the initial value, the terminal value, and the step value in the following flowchart symbol?

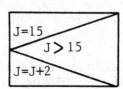
    ```

3. Explain why the following FOR/NEXT loops are invalid, then indicate how to correct each loop.

a.   10 FOR I = 10 TO 1 STEP 0

.

.

.

50 NEXT I

b.   10 FOR J = 1 TO 5
20   LET J = J / 2
30   PRINT J
40 NEXT J

c.   10 FOR K = 1 TO 10 STEP -2
20   LET T = K + 4
30 NEXT K

4. Write transfer instructions to meet the folowing requirements:

a.   Test to see if test score (T) is greater than 70. If so, print name (N$) and PASSING GRADE.

b.   Execute a loop 10 times to print your name end to end (for instance, RonRonRon . . . Ron).

5.   What is the final value of X in the following program module?

```
100 LET X = 0
110 READ A
120 WHILE A <> 0
130     PRINT A,X
140     X = X + A
150     READ A
160 WEND
170 DATA 1,3,4,0
999 END
```

6.   Given the flowchart below, write the corresponding BASIC code (use a WHILE/WEND loop).

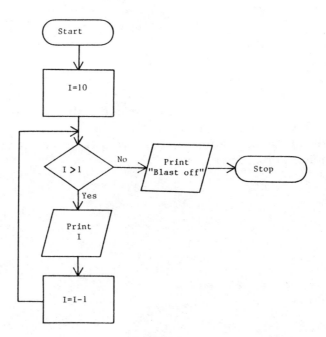

7. Write the corresponding BASIC code for the flowchart in Question 6, but in this case use a FOR/NEXT loop.

8. Write a program section that will sum the first 100 even integers and then will print the total.

9. Write a program section to count and print the total number of senior citizens and their average age. (NOTE: Use a flag at the end of the data).

10. What is wrong with the following program segment? How can the code be corrected.

```
10 READ N$
20 WHILE N$ <> " LAST"
30          READ ADDRESS$
40          PRINT "Name: ";N$
50 PRINT "Address: ";ADDRESS$
60 NEXT N$
70 DATA "SARA","700 JACKSON ST",
80 DATA "JANET","473 MERCER RD"
99 END
```

PROGRAMMING PROBLEM 1

Write a program that reads an integer i and makes the following calculation:

$$i + (i - 1) + (i - 2) + \ldots + (\text{until integer} = 1) =$$

For example, if the integer read is 6, the output will look like this:

$$6 + 5 + 4 + 3 + 2 + 1 = 21$$

PROGRAMMING PROBLEM 1 (cont.)

PROGRAMMING PROBLEM 2

Andy is trying to learn his multiplication tables. His father would like you to write a program to help teach Andy these tables. The program should permit Andy to input any number into the program. The computer will print the equations and answers to that number when it is multiplied by the numbers 1 through 9. The program should continue prompting Andy to enter new numbers until he decides to end the program.

The output should be similar to the following:

Multiplication Table for Number X

    X * 1 = XXX
    X * 2 = XXX
        .
        .
        .
    X * 9 = XXX

PROGRAMMING PROBLEM 2 (cont.)

ANSWER KEY

Worksheet

Your answers for the odd worksheet questions should contain most of the information below. Questions requiring specific responses should match the answers given below.

1. a.   10   20   30   THAT'S ALL

     b. $*$*$*$*

  c.   6
        5
        4
        3
        2
        1

3. a.   Step 0 causes an infinite loop to occur; the program needs a negative step of at least 1.

```
10 FOR I = 10 TO 1 STEP -1
     .
     .
     .
50 NEXT I
```

     b.   A loop control variable should never be modified within the body of the loop.

```
10 FOR J = 1 TO 5
20      LET K = J / 2
30      PRINT K
40 NEXT J
```

     c.   This loop has a negative step value. Thus, the loop never will execute.

```
10 FOR K = 1 TO 10 STEP 2
20      LET T = K + 4
30 NEXT K
```

5. The final value of X is 8.

7.
```
10 FOR I = 10 TO 1 STEP - 1
20              PRINT I
30 NEXT I
40 PRINT "BLAST-OFF"
99 END
```

9. ```
     10 READ AGE
     20 WHILE AGE > 65
     30   LET COUNT = COUNT + 1
     40   LET TOTAL = TOTAL + AGE
     50   READ AGE
     60 WEND
     70 AVERAGE = TOTAL / COUNT
     80 PRINT "COUNT =";COUNT
     90 PRINT "AVERAGE AGE =";AVERAGE
     100 DATA 72,84,69,70,68,82,90,72,63
     999 END
```
```

Solution to Programming Problem 1

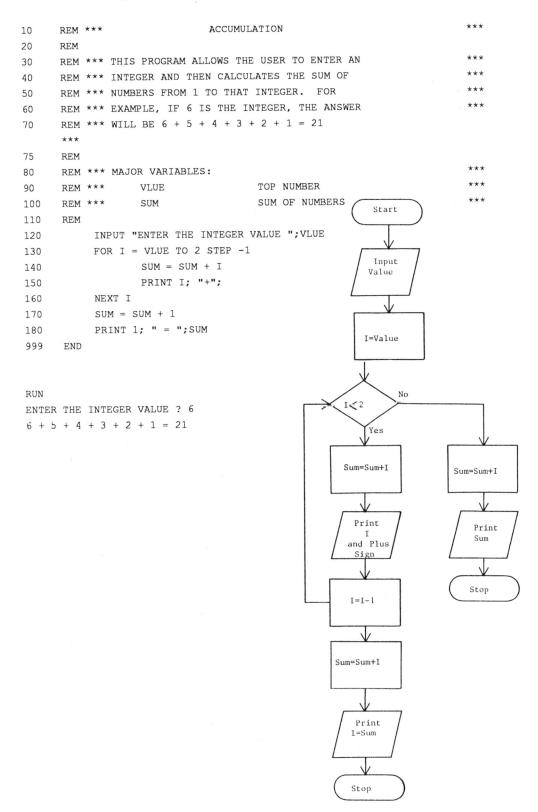

```
10      REM ***                    ACCUMULATION                              ***
20      REM
30      REM *** THIS PROGRAM ALLOWS THE USER TO ENTER AN          ***
40      REM *** INTEGER AND THEN CALCULATES THE SUM OF            ***
50      REM *** NUMBERS FROM 1 TO THAT INTEGER.  FOR              ***
60      REM *** EXAMPLE, IF 6 IS THE INTEGER, THE ANSWER          ***
70      REM *** WILL BE 6 + 5 + 4 + 3 + 2 + 1 = 21
        ***
75      REM
80      REM *** MAJOR VARIABLES:                                  ***
90      REM ***     VLUE                TOP NUMBER                ***
100     REM ***     SUM                 SUM OF NUMBERS            ***
110     REM
120         INPUT "ENTER THE INTEGER VALUE ";VLUE
130         FOR I = VLUE TO 2 STEP -1
140             SUM = SUM + I
150             PRINT I; "+";
160         NEXT I
170         SUM = SUM + 1
180         PRINT 1; " = ";SUM
999     END


RUN
ENTER THE INTEGER VALUE ? 6
6 + 5 + 4 + 3 + 2 + 1 = 21
```

Section V
The Decision Statement and Functions

SUMMARY

All BASIC programs consist of some statements that are normally executed in sequential order. However, branching can be used to alter the flow of execution or bypass certain instructions. The GOSUB statement is used for branching. When a GOSUB statement appears, the program is instructed to go to the first line of the appropriate subroutine. The GOSUB statement, when it is used alone, is an unconditional transfer statement because the flow of execution always is altered when the statement is encountered. When a RETURN statement is encountered, program control returns to the line immediately following the GOSUB statement.

Using GOSUB statements can eliminate the need to repeat sections of code. Instead, code can be placed within a subroutine, then called for execution as often as it is required to support processing.

The IF statement causes a conditional transfer; its effect on the path of program execution depends on whether a specific condition or conditions are met. There are two variations of the IF statement: the single-alternative IF statement (IF/THEN) and the double-alternative IF statement (IF/THEN/ELSE).

A single-alternative IF statement tests a condition; if the condition is true, the action stated after the THEN part of the statement is executed; if it is false, no action is taken and program execution simply continues on to the next statement. The double-alternative variation of the IF statement also tests a condition. If the condition is true, the action stated after the THEN part of the statement is executed and the ELSE is ignored; if it is false, the action after the ELSE part of the statement is executed and the THEN portion is ignored. IF statements can be used in combination with GOSUB statements. When this is done, the GOSUB forms part of a conditional transfer statement.

Some standard library functions have been built into the BASIC language and are included in the BASIC language library, where the programmer can reference them easily. These functions perform frequently used arithmetic routines. The argument is a value used by the function to obtain a result and can consist of a constant, a variable, a mathematical expression, or another function. These functions are used in place of constants, variables, or expressions in BASIC statements.

The definition statement allows the programmer to define a function not already included in the BASIC language. The DEF statement can be placed anywhere before the first reference to it. The function name consists of the letters FN followed by any valid numeric variable name. The expression can contain any mathematical operations desired.

STRUCTURED LEARNING

DIRECTIONS: *First, use a blank sheet of paper to cover the answer, without reading it. Then read the question carefully and write the letter of the correct answer in the space provided. Uncover the answer to see if you chose the correct response.*

1. In BASIC, an example of an unconditional transfer statement is the

_____ .

a.   END statement
b.   IF/THEN statement
c.   GOSUB statement
d.   FOR/NEXT statement

c.   GOSUB. Unconditional transfer statements cause a branch in the flow of execution every time they are encountered. In BASIC, the GOSUB statement meets this criterion. (Although the GOSUB statement can be part of a THEN statement within an IF/THEN pair, the GOSUB is never really encountered if the THEN condition is not executed.)

2. Which of the following are invalid IF/THEN statements?
a.   10 IF J = 10
       THEN 60
b.   10 IF N = "END"
       THEN 60
c.   10 IF X < Y
       THEN 40
d.   10 IF J$ = NONE
       THEN 100

b and d. In forming comparison statements, you must compare like items; for example, character strings must be compared

with string variables, and numeric values must be compared
with numeric variables.

3. In BASIC, the argument of a function can be _____ .

a.   a variable
b.   another function
c.   a mathematical expression
d.   all of the above

◊ ◊ ◊ ◊ ◊ ◊ ◊ ◊ ◊ ◊ ◊ ◊ ◊ ◊ ◊ ◊ ◊ ◊

d.   All of the above. An argument is a value used by the function to
obtain results, and therefore can be any of the above—and also
can be a constant—depending on the use for the function.

4. The DEF statement can be placed _____ .

a.   after the reference to a function
b.   anywhere before the first reference to a function
c.   only on the line immediately preceding the reference to a function
d.   anywhere in a program

◊ ◊ ◊ ◊ ◊ ◊ ◊ ◊ ◊ ◊ ◊ ◊ ◊ ◊ ◊ ◊ ◊ ◊

b.   After a function has been defined, the programmer can refer to it
whenever necessary; therefore, the DEF statement must come
before the first reference to the function.

5. If the condition after the IF in an IF/THEN statement is false, control is transferred to _____ .

a.   the end of the program
b.   the line following the word THEN
c.   the next statement in the program
d.   the statement following the word ELSE

◊ ◊ ◊ ◊ ◊ ◊ ◊ ◊ ◊ ◊ ◊ ◊ ◊ ◊ ◊ ◊ ◊ ◊

c.   If the condition tested is true, the action after the THEN part of
the statement is executed; if the condition is false, no action is
taken and program execution simply continues to the next
statement in sequence.

WORKSHEET

1. What will happen in line 60 in the following section of code?

   40 LET X = X + 5
   50 PRINT X
   60 IF X < 10
   GOSUB 100

   .
   .
   .

   99 END

   100 LET X = X - 5
   110 PRINT X

   .
   .
   .

   400 RETURN

2. Given the following flowchart, write the necessary code.

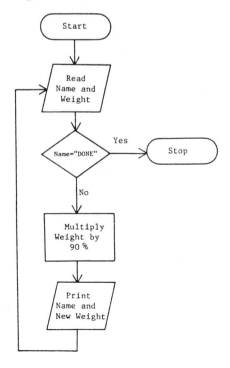

3. Write a line of code to define the following function:
    $(X + 5 \wedge 2) * 3 / 4$

    Name the function FNA

4. What is wrong with this program? How can it be corrected?
    ```
    10 LET A = 2
    20 PRINT A
    40 IF A < 10
          THEN GOSUB 60
    50 LET A = A + 2
    60 RETURN
    99 END
    ```

5. What is the output of the following program?
    ```
    10 LET C = 1
    20 GOSUB 100
    99END

    100 WHILE C < 4
    110    LET N$ = "Let it Snow"
    120    PRINT N$
    130    LET C = C + 1
    140 WEND
    150 RETURN
    ```

6. What is the final value of X?

```
100 READ A
110 LET X = 0
120 GOSUB 1000
130 DATA 1,3,4,0
999 END

1000   WHILE A <> 0
1010       LET X = X + 1
1020       PRINT A,X
1030   WEND
1040   RETUR
```

7. What would be the output for the following two program segments?

a.
```
10 DATA 3,2,0,1
20 READ X
30 GOSUB 100
99 END
100 WHILE X <> 1
110 PRINT X
120 READ X
130 WEND
140 RETURN
```

b.
```
10 READ "RON","PAT","END"
20 READ N$
30 IF N$ = "END"
    THEN 99
40 PRINT N$
99 END
```

8. What will happen when the following code is encountered? Assume
    that N$ = Melissa.

          120 IF N$ = "END"
             THEN PRINT "THAT'S ALL"
             ELSE PRINT "NAME:";N$

9. _____ are functions defined by the programmer that are not already
    included in the BASIC language library.

10. What limitations, if any, are placed on the length of a function
    definition?

STUDY GUIDE   B-59

PROGRAMMING PROBLEM 1

Your school is presenting its first play of the season this weekend. Ticket sales have been booming. The principal would like a report listing total sales to date, as well as the sales for each different type of ticket. The types of tickets, their prices, and the number sold of each are:

Type	Price	Sold
Adults	$3.55	206
Senior Citizens	$3.15	33
Students	$1.75	105
Children	$1.05	103

The report should be similar to the following:

TICKET SALES

TYPE	PRICE	SALES
ADULTS	$ 3.55	$ 731.30
SENIORS	$ 3.15	$ 103.95
STUDENTS	$ 1.75	$ 183.75
CHILDREN	$ 1.05	$ 108.15
TOTAL SALES		$ 1127.15

PROGRAMMING PROBLEM 1 (cont.)

PROGRAMMING PROBLEM 2

Write a program to find the number of quarters, nickels, and pennies required to equal a given amount of change, using the smallest possible number of coins.

PROGRAMMING PROBLEM 2 (cont.)

ANSWER KEY

Worksheet

Your answers for the odd worksheet questions should contain most of the information below. Questions requiring specific responses should match the answers given below.

1. Line 60 will be executed if X is less than 10. If so, the program will branch to line 100.

3. 10 DEF FNA(X) = (X + 5 ^ 2) * 3 / 4

5. Let it Snow
   Let it Snow
   Let it Snow

7. a. output: 3 2
   b. output: RON

9. User-defined functions

Solution to Programming Problem 1

```
10      REM ***                         TICKET SALES                    ***
20      REM
30      REM *** THIS PROGRAM COMPUTES TICKET SALES BY                    ***
40      REM *** TICKET TYPE AND BY GRAND TOTAL.                          ***
45      REM
50      REM *** MAJOR VARIABLES:                                         ***
60      REM ***        TYPE          TICKET TYPE                         ***
70      REM ***        PRICE         PRICE PER TICKET                    ***
80      REM ***        SOLD          NUMBER OF TICKETS SOLD              ***
90      REM ***        SUB           SUBTOTAL OF SALES/TYPE              ***
100     REM ***        GRND          GRAND TOTAL SALES                   ***
110     REM
120     REM 1.0 PRINT THE HEADINGS
125     REM
130         PRINT,"TICKET SALES"
140         PRINT
150         PRINT "TYPE:,"PRICE","SALES"
160         PRINT "----","-----","-----"
170         PRINT
180         GOSUB 1000
185     REM
190     REM 3.0 PRINT THE GRAND TOTAL
195     REM
200         PRINT,,"-------"
210         PRINT "TOTAL SALES",,"$";GRND
220     REM
230     REM 4.0 DATA STATEMENTS
235     REM
240         DATA ADULTS,3.55,206
250         DATA SENIORS,3.15,33
260         DATA STUDENTS,1.75,105
270         DATA CHILDREN,1.05,103
280         DATA LAST,0,0
999     END

1000    REM 2.0 READ THE TICKET TYPE, PRICE, AND
        NUMBER SOLD
1010    REM
1020        WHILE TICKETS$ <> "LAST"
1030          SUBTTAL = PRICE * SOLD
1040          GRND = GRND + SUBTTAL
1050          PRINT TICKET$,"$";PRICE,"$"SUBTTAL
1060          READ TICKET$,PRICE,SOLD
1070        WEND
1080        RETURN

RUN
            TICKET SALES

TYPE            PRICE           SALES
--------        -----           ------
ADULTS          $ 3.55          $  731.30
SENIORS         $ 3.15          $  103.95
STUDENTS        $ 1.75          $  183.75
CHILDREN        $ 1.05          $  108.15
                                ----------
TOTAL SALES                     $ 1127.15
```